Go

How to Master Online Learning

About Peterson's
To succeed on your lifelong educational journey, you will need accurate, dependable, and practical tools and resources. That is why Peterson's is everywhere education happens. Because whenever and however you need education content delivered, you can rely on Peterson's to provide the information, know-how, and guidance to help you reach your goals. Tools to match the right students with the right school. It's here. Personalized resources and expert guidance. It's here. Comprehensive and dependable education content—delivered whenever and however you need it. It's all here.

For more information, contact Peterson's, 2000 Lenox Drive, Lawrenceville, NJ 08648; 800-338-3282 Ext. 54229.

© 2010 Peterson's, a Nelnet company

Stephen Clemente, Managing Director, Publishing and Institutional Research; Bernadette Webster, Director of Publishing; Mark D. Snider, Editor; Ray Golaszewski, Publishing Operations Manager; Linda M. Williams, Composition Manager

ISBN-13: 978-0-7689-3308-6
ISBN-10: 0-7689-3308-8

Printed in Canada

10 9 8 7 6 5 4 3 2 1   12 11 10

First Edition

By producing this book on recycled paper (40% post consumer waste) 27 trees were saved.

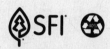

Certified Chain of Custody

60% Certified Fiber Sourcing and
40% Post-Consumer Recycled

www.sfiprogram.org

*This label applies to the text stock.

Sustainability—Its Importance to Peterson's, a Nelnet company

What does sustainability mean to Peterson's? As a leading publisher, we are aware that our business has a direct impact on vital resources—most especially the trees that are used to make our books. Peterson's is proud that its products are certified by the Sustainable Forestry Initiative (SFI) and that all of its books are printed on paper that is 40 percent post-consumer waste.

Being a part of the Sustainable Forestry Initiative (SFI) means that all of our vendors—from paper suppliers to printers—have undergone rigorous audits to demonstrate that they are maintaining a sustainable environment.

Peterson's continually strives to find new ways to incorporate sustainability throughout all aspects of its business.

Go

Contents

Acknowledgments

We would like to thank the following people and organizations for their permission to reproduce course materials:

Professor Moises F. Salinas, Central Connecticut State University, for his course overview and syllabus for Psychology 112.

www.StudentAffairs.com for allowing us to adapt its evaluation form.

Mark A. Davenport, The University of North Carolina at Greensboro, for his course overview and syllabus, "A Student Affairs Professional's Guide to Data Reporting Using SPSS for Windows."

Development: Practical Strategies, LLC: Reyna Eisenstark, Margaret C. Moran

Find Definitions of Underlined Terms

Find definitions of key terms in Appendix: Some Online Learning Terms You Should Know. Peterson's has underlined key terms throughout this book that may be unfamiliar to new online learners. You can find out what these terms mean by searching alphabetically through our appendix at the back of the book.

Find Us on Facebook® & Follow Us on Twitter™

Join the Online Learning conversation on Facebook® and Twitter™ at www.facebook.com/studyremotely and www.twitter. com/studyremotely and receive additional test-prep tips and advice. Peterson's resources are available to help you do your best on this important exam—and others in your future.

Peterson's publishes a full line of books—test prep, education exploration, financial aid, and career preparation. Peterson's publications can be found at high school guidance offices, college libraries and career centers, and your local bookstore and library. Peterson's books are now also available as eBooks.

We welcome any comments or suggestions you may have about this publication. Your feedback will help us make educational dreams possible for you—and others like you.

▶Part I

LOOKING AT ONLINE OPTIONS

Search

Chapter 1 `Go`

Is Online Learning Right for You?

. . . .

"I believe that effective instruction (online or otherwise) is student-centered, rather than teacher-centered. This means that you—the student—are responsible for your own learning and success. If you are highly motivated, log on and participate at least six times in each course unit, and produce high-quality work, you will be successful. However, if you log on sporadically, participate minimally, or submit poor quality work, you will not. Online higher education is aimed at independent learners. If you require the structure of a classroom, then online courses will not suit you."

Alexandra M. Pickett
Associate Director, SUNY Learning Network, SUNY System Administration
Adjunct Professor, State University of New York at Albany

. . . .

WHAT IS ONLINE LEARNING?

Google the term "online learning" and you're likely to come up with over a million hits, which is overwhelming. How can you use all the information available to figure out just what online learning is and whether you should venture into it?

The best place to begin is with the basics. Simply put, online learning is a type of education in which the majority of instruction occurs on the computer via the Internet. An online course might use any or all of the following technologies: Web cameras, live chat, discussion boards, podcasting, and instant messaging.

HOW WE GOT HERE: A BRIEF HISTORY

You might have noticed that online learning is also referred to as distance learning. This is because most or all of the education takes place at a location some distance from a bricks-and-mortar school. In fact, some "schools"—for-profit educational entities—are only virtual institutions. Although online learning is a relatively new concept that emerged with the Internet, distance learning has been around for over a hundred years.

Correspondence Courses

The earliest form of distance learning involved sending materials back and forth through the mail. These kinds of correspondence courses became popular in the United States beginning in the late 1800s. One of the earliest correspondence courses taught shorthand. Students would copy passages and send them to an instructor by mail who graded and returned the work to the student.

Correspondence courses became a way for people who could not otherwise attend school to get an education. This included people with disabilities, women who were not allowed to enroll in most colleges, people who worked during school hours, and people who lived in remote areas of the country where there were no schools.

The Next Big Thing

Television eventually became a new forum for distance learning. By the late 1970s, some colleges and universities began using cable and satellite television for distance education courses. Often, the courses were offered early in the morning before people went to work or their children got up.

The Move to Online Learning

With the growth of the Internet in the 1990s, online learning was the obvious next step. Initially, teachers at colleges and universities used it just to post things online for the entire class to download such as the course schedule or list of readings. They found it a more efficient way to provide routine information.

Eventually, however, schools began to consider online learning as a way to serve students and professionals who did not have access to a campus or the time to take courses on a traditional class schedule. Though on-campus evening and weekend classes were available, this was not always an option for adult students with families. Online learning seemed the perfect solution. As technology improved in the late 1990s, so did the number of online course offerings.

ONLINE LEARNING TAKES OFF

The first attempts at online education met with resistance from traditional educators. Many insisted that an instructor was necessary for the educational process and that online classes lacking traditional structure were inferior. As a result of this backlash, many employers came to share the same opinion. Often, when choosing between two otherwise equally qualified candidates, employers would be more likely to prefer the person who had earned a traditional degree rather than an online degree.

This notion has changed radically in recent years, mostly because of people's increasing familiarity with personal computers, which have entered nearly every aspect of public and private life. It is estimated that today around 207 million Americans are already quite comfortable with a popular form of asynchronous online communication: the Internet.

As use of the Internet has grown since the 1990s, traditional colleges and universities across the country have introduced and expanded their online programs. Offerings include everything from a single course on travel writing to online accredited degree programs in child psychology. In addition, many professionals who need to take continuing education courses to maintain their certifications or licensures find plenty of these courses offered online. It is possible to speculate that one day the online degree may be the one that is more common.

The Future Is NOW

Taking a course online is in many ways similar to taking a course in a traditional face-to-face classroom setting. There is an instructor, a syllabus outlining the topics the course will cover, and expectations for the class, which include participating in discussions, taking examinations, and writing papers. The main difference between an online course and a traditional course is that students may do all these things without ever entering a classroom. Many students will complete a course entirely from their own homes—and some will complete it at their own pace.

Today, the number of students taking at least one online course each semester is growing at a faster rate than the growth of overall enrollments in postsecondary institutions. According to "Staying the Course: Online Education in the United States 2008," a report from the Sloan Consortium, an organization that studies and supports online learning, 3.9 million students took an online class in the fall of 2007. According to the National Center for Education Statistics (NCES), the number had been only 1.6 million students five years earlier. In *Projections of Education Statistics to 2017*, NCES estimates that more than three-quarters of all higher education students will be taking online courses by 2017.

WHO OFFERS ONLINE LEARNING?

Where can you find an online course? Just about anywhere.

Studies by NCES have found that large public educational institutions generally have the greatest number of online offerings and the most positive attitude toward <u>online learning</u>. But many other schools have become aware that online programs may rival the offerings of traditional programs and that <u>online learning</u> offers real competition in attracting students. As a result, more schools, including private ones, have begun to shift their attitude toward <u>online learning</u> in order to appeal to the increasing numbers of nontraditional students looking for educational opportunities, especially in the area of job preparation. Community colleges, technical institutes, and trade associations are leaders in this area.

The Sloan Consortium reported in its 2005 study "Growing by Degrees" that by fall 2004, 44 percent of schools offering traditional master's degree programs also offered online master's programs. Online associate degree programs and certificate programs were the next most common offerings, with nearly 40 percent of schools offering online associate degrees and about 35 percent offering online certificates.

In addition to traditional schools that offer online versions of their degree or certificate programs, there are also virtual colleges, universities, and training schools that exist solely online. These institutions offer online degree programs as well as continuing education credits, diplomas, and certificates. So if you are interested in an online course, program, or degree, you won't have far to look.

TYPES OF ONLINE LEARNING

Online courses can be as different as traditional classroom-based courses. Some are highly interactive, utilizing various forms of technology, whereas others follow a more traditional model, in which instructors present lectures online and students must prepare written responses. In some online courses, nearly all the content is delivered online, with no meetings between students and instructors. In others, much of the content is delivered online, but there might be one or two face-to-face meetings in a classroom. There might also be on-campus lab hours.

Synchronous Learning

Some online classes are synchronous, which means "at the same time." In this type of online learning, students and instructors, wherever they are geographically located, log in to a Web site at the same time. There, instructors can give lectures, students and instructors can participate in classroom discussions, and cooperative projects can take place in real time. These classes approximate face-to-face classroom experiences, such as lectures or group meetings, by using technology such as Webcasting, chat rooms, and virtual classrooms.

One benefit of this kind of online learning is that students receive instant feedback. If someone makes a comment or asks a question, he or she can be answered immediately by an instructor or by the other students—similar to a traditional classroom. Groups of students can also work together on projects at the same time.

In general, synchronous learning tends to work best for those students who can schedule set days and times to work on their studies. For example, each Tuesday from 6:00–9:00 p.m., you must be ready to log online to your class and participate. Students who thrive with more structure may prefer synchronous learning because it is closer to a face-to-face class in terms of everyone being present at the same time.

However, one disadvantage of synchronous learning is that it takes place in real time. It does not allow students to work at their own pace. You must always be available on the same days and times, and you must be prepared to participate at those times. If you need more time to work on something, you may not have the opportunity.

Asynchronous Learning

If your schedule is a reason you're considering online learning, then an asynchronous course may be a better option for you. In an asynchronous course, communication between students and instructors does not happen in real time. Students can work at their own pace, posting messages to various discussion groups, and exchanging e-mails with one another and the instructor whenever it's most convenient for them. Although students in these courses are expected to interact with the instructor and other students regularly, interaction may be done at any time—within the time frame of the course. You might have readings to do, projects to complete, and online quizzes or tests, but these can all be accomplished when you're ready for them. Asynchronous courses also rely on technology, which may include e-mail, message boards, and prerecorded video lectures.

Asynchronous learning can work well for students with complicated schedules who may not have the same time available each day or week and who like to work at their own pace. Some students might want to complete all the assignments during a single week when they have more time, and others might pace themselves to complete the work over a period of weeks.

This type of online learning usually works best for students who are self-motivated. If this doesn't describe your learning style, it can make asynchronous learning a challenge because it is much easier to put off doing course work when you don't have weekly deadlines to meet. In addition, asynchronous learning does not offer instant feedback so you may have to wait to have questions or concerns addressed.

Blended or Hybrid Learning

When you're looking into courses, you may find that the one you're interested in combines synchronous and asynchronous interactions. In addition, some courses might include occasional face-to-face interactions. This is known as blended learning, or hybrid learning, literally a blend of traditional classroom or lab interactions with online activities such as e-mail, discussion boards, online tests, and announcements.

Evaluating the Options

It is important to consider both your learning style and your schedule when deciding among synchronous, asynchronous, and blended online courses. If you feel isolated studying by yourself or prefer to work closely with your instructor and other students in the class, synchronous courses may be a better choice than asynchronous courses. If you cannot commit to specific class times because of work or other obligations, you might consider asynchronous learning. Depending on your needs, hybrid courses may present the same problem as synchronous courses.

WHAT ARE ONLINE COURSES LIKE?

The one thing that is generally true for every online course, whether asynchronous, synchronous, or blended, is that there will be a considerable amount of reading to do, in which you will be asked to respond either in writing or in an online discussion.

Some courses also involve virtual group projects in which you and your classmates work together on a project online. Other courses may require a group presentation in which each person in the group presents one part of a project that you have completed together.

INSTRUCTORS AND ONLINE LEARNING

Because the type of <u>online learning</u> differs from course to course and even class to class, it's no surprise that the instructor's role may be different, too.

Instructor-Led Courses

In instructor-led online courses, which are most like traditional courses, students are led through the class material by an instructor. He or she develops a curriculum, sets up a course schedule, gives assignments, leads discussions, answers student questions, and assigns grades at the end of the course. All the students in the course learn at the same time and participate in discussions together.

Instructor-Facilitated Courses

In instructor-facilitated online courses, instructors guide the process, but students learn mostly on their own. Students use textbooks, course videos, and other online resources as their major sources of information and instruction. Students participate in online discussions with classmates, but these may take place at various times. The instructor provides feedback on all assignments.

Self-Paced Learning

Self-paced learning, or independent study, involves no interaction with instructors or other students. In these types of courses, students are directed to the course materials and are then expected to learn independently by following their own schedule. Most self-paced courses do not have a start and end date. Instead, students begin the course and progress through the course materials at their own pace. These courses usually require the greatest amount of self-discipline because you are the only one to set your schedule for completing assignments and finishing the course.

▶ SAMPLE COURSE OVERVIEW AND SYLLABUS

Here is the course outline for a psychology course offered by Professor Moises F. Salinas at Central Connecticut State University during a summer semester. The outline details the course objectives, what the students are expected to complete, and how the class is structured. The course is <u>asynchronous</u>. Students were expected to complete the work for each unit on their own schedule, but within a certain time frame.

PSYCHOLOGY 112

I. OVERVIEW
Welcome to the PSY 112 Online course. I know that for many of you, this will be your first experience taking an online course, but I am sure we will have a great experience. These are the instructions regarding the way this course is going to work. I designed it to give you maximum flexibility regarding time and dates. You can complete each unit at your leisure as long as you have completed Unit 6 by the date of the midterm (see <u>syllabus</u>) and the rest of the units by the date of the second test. I do recommend, however, that you set a structured schedule because students who do are usually more successful taking online courses.

OBJECTIVES
At the end of this course the student will:

1. Have a deeper understanding of himself/herself.

2. Know the fundamentals of human behavior.

3. Appreciate the diversity of human behavior.

4. Use the acquired knowledge in making simple analyses of human behavior.

5. Desire to expand his/her knowledge of psychology.

II. COURSE MATERIALS

Required Texts:
Exploring Psychology (4th Edition), by David G. Myers
How to Write Psychology Papers, Parrot, L. (1999).

Optional:
Study Guide that accompanies the text.

III. COURSE REQUIREMENTS

A. Class Performance: For each unit, the student will read the assigned book chapter. This allows the student to become familiar with concepts to be discussed and provides time for forethought in formulating pertinent questions for clarification or discussion. The student will then complete the assigned online exercises. Full completion of the exercises will count for 10 percent of the grade.

B. Threaded Discussion: After reading the assigned chapter and completing the exercise, each participant will be required to participate with at least *two postings* in that unit's threaded discussions. I have posted a question for each unit to begin the discussion, but you should read the postings of all your classmates and you can add comments to their postings as well as answer the question. Completing this requirement by posting at least two relevant comments per unit will earn you 10 percent of the final grade.

C. Exams: One midterm and one final exam, each worth 15 percent of your final grade, will be given online and *available only for the posted date.* The exams will consist of objectively scored items (multiple choice, true/false).

D. Comprehensive Take-Home Final: A take-home final of five open-ended questions. This exam will be individual, available online one week before the end of the session and due on the last day of class. The test will be worth 30 percent of your grade.

E. Reaction Papers: Two 1–2 page papers stating your opinion about any subject discussed in class. Each is worth 10 percent of your grade. The first paper can be turned in at any point before the midterm, and the second paper can be turned in at any point before the final. However, I encourage you not to wait until the two final weeks to submit the reaction papers.

F. Evaluation: Your final grade will be based upon the following:

Midterm Exam	15%
Final Exam	15%
Take Home	30%
2 Reaction Papers	20%
Exercise Participation	10%
Threaded Discussion Participation	10%

Letter Grade Conversion:

90% to 100%	A
80% to 89%	B
70% to 79%	C
60% to 69%	D
59% or less	F

IV. STUDENTS WITH SPECIAL NEEDS

If a student has any special needs, it is *the student's responsibility to notify me at the beginning of the semester* so special arrangements can be made. No special arrangements will be made after the 12th day of class.

COURSE SYLLABUS

UNIT	SCHEDULE	READINGS & ASSIGNMENTS
1	Introduction to Psychology	Chapter 1
2	Biopsychology	Chapter 2
3	Developmental	Chapter 3
4	Intelligence	Chapter 8
5	Consciousness	Chapter 5
6	Learning	Chapter 6
	Midterm	
7	Cognition	Chapter 7
8	Emotion & Stress	Chapter 10 *Hypothesis Due*
9	Personality	Chapter 11
10	Abnormal Psychology	Chapter 12
11	Therapy I	Chapter 13 *References Due*
12	Social	Chapter 14
	Final Exam	*Term Papers Due*

WHO ARE ONLINE LEARNERS?

. . . .

"I loved my online experience! I liked the fact that I was able to complete and submit the work on my own time. As long as you're a self-motivated individual, I think online classes are a great option. I got the courses that I need to graduate without the commitment of a scheduled class time, which I really enjoyed and needed because of my work schedule."

Tiffany Millen
Nutrition Major, 2011
Rutgers, The State University of New Jersey

. . . .

Millions of Americans have chosen <u>online learning</u> in order to earn a degree, receive continuing education credits, further their professional and trade skills, or learn something new. But just who are these online learners?

Online learners are a diverse group. They come in a wide range of ages, occupations, backgrounds, previous educational experience, and interests. They take online courses for a variety of reasons. An online learner might be a single parent completing an associate degree, a teacher earning CEUs (continuing education units) to retain his or her license, or someone working full-time and pursuing an MBA program, studying at night and on the weekends. An online learner might be a U.S. soldier overseas pursuing a college degree or a student taking AP physics from a virtual high school because her high school doesn't offer the course.

Nontraditional Students

Over the past twenty years, the number of adult students returning to college or attending college for the first time has steadily increased. These adult students make up a large percentage of today's online learners. In fact, according to the 2008 report "Staying the Course" by the Sloan Consortium, over half of all online students are pursuing associate's degrees.

Filling in a Course Requirement

Some online learners are students who are already enrolled in a degree program at a traditional college or university. They might take online courses in addition to their usual course load during the fall and winter semesters or over the summer so they can receive their degrees in a shorter amount of time. Students also sign up for courses offered online because they can't fit the traditional courses into their regular college schedules.

Overcoming Distance

A student interested in a particular course, degree program, or certification might not be able to find it on a nearby campus or might not find a local program that fits his or her schedule. However, an online offering may solve the problem. It certainly solves the problem for men and women in the military earning their degrees as they move from post to post or serve abroad.

Students with Disabilities

Online learning can also be a good option for students with disabilities. Students who have hearing or vision loss can work with various forms of technology such as closed captioning or screen readers to help them participate in online learning programs.

Lifelong Learning

While online courses can help people earn degrees and certifications, these courses can also satisfy the desire of people to remain lifelong learners. In addition to offering courses that confer credit, a variety of online sources such as universities, museums, and businesses offer noncredit courses that people enroll in simply to learn about things that interest them—from Renaissance art to black holes.

WILL ONLINE LEARNING WORK FOR YOU?

Today, with advances in computer technology and greater access to the Internet, it's easy to see how online learning in theory can work for just about anyone. Students are no longer limited by such factors as physical or learning disabilities, geographic locations, or socioeconomic status. When you're learning online, the playing field is level.

However, it's important to realize that online learning may not be the right option for everyone. Some people may have limited access to the Internet, and some might struggle with learning and using new forms of technology. Others may find the amount of reading and writing to be overwhelming or may feel uncomfortable with online discussions. Still others may not be able to structure their time around their course work or may lack support from their families. Many of these obstacles can be overcome, and the rewards of an online degree or certification are very likely to be worth it.

Testing the Idea

One way to get your feet wet without making a big commitment is to take a single online course. In this way, you will be able to get a sense of the amount of work required, learn how to use the online technology, and figure out how to fit schoolwork into the rest of your life. If the initial online course is taken for credit, you'll be able to apply it to your degree.

▶ IS ONLINE LEARNING RIGHT FOR YOU? CHECKLIST

Complete this checklist and see if online learning might work for you. Are you prepared to . . .

- ☐ participate in a virtual classroom three to five days a week?
- ☐ have access to the necessary equipment—a computer and modem with high-speed Internet access?
- ☐ be comfortable with new forms of technology?
- ☐ be able to complete online assignments on time?
- ☐ communicate regularly and comfortably through writing?
- ☐ respond to other students' ideas and questions in writing or through a chat room?
- ☐ have the discipline necessary to keep up with course work?
- ☐ have a private space to log in for classes and assignments as well as a private space to study?
- ☐ If you have checked off all or most of these questions, online learning may be just the answer to continuing your education!

Truth or Myth: The Facts About Online Learning

. . . .

"The academic library at my online university is wonderful. I have access to a huge number of databases. That may be true for schools with actual physical campuses, but the online nature of the work forces us to constantly use the library to retrieve scholarly articles."

Joe Rosenfeld
MS, Mental Health Counseling, 2013
Walden University

. . . .

What does the term "online learning" mean to you? You may think you already know what it is. You may have heard about it from others who have taken online courses, or you might have your own ideas about what goes on in a course based on your own experience with computers and having gone to bricks-and-mortar schools.

TRUTHS AND MYTHS ABOUT ONLINE LEARNING

Some of what you have heard about online learning may be correct. But once you actually start an online course, you may find that it is very different from what you expected. It is important to separate the myths from the facts about online learning before you decide to enroll in online programs.

► TRUE OR FALSE: THE ONLINE LEARNING QUIZ

Here are some common beliefs about <u>online learning</u>. See if you can separate the facts from the myths.

___T ___F <u>Online learning</u> classes are easier than traditional face-to-face classes.

___T ___F You don't need to be a computer whiz to take online courses.

___T ___F There is very little interaction between students and teachers in online courses.

___T ___F <u>Online learning</u> courses are less effective than traditional classroom instruction.

___T ___F Online classes are of lower quality than traditional classes.

___T ___F There is much less reading to do for online courses.

___T ___F Online classes are much cheaper than traditional classes.

___T ___F All online courses are the same quality.

___T ___F <u>Online learning</u> is really for people who don't live near colleges.

___T ___F Cheating is easy online.

___T ___F Most employers don't approve of or accept online degrees.

___T ___F You can do all your course work for online classes at the last minute.

How did you do on the quiz? Let's take a look at the truth about <u>online learning</u>. You may be surprised at what you find out about your perception of <u>online learning</u>.

MYTH: Online Learning Is Easy

MYTH: Online Courses Have Less Reading

MYTH: Course work Can Be Done at the Last Minute

False: That online courses are easy and its variants about the amount of work involved are the most common myths about online learning. It's true that it's fairly easy to access an online class, either as a student or as an instructor. All you need to get started is a computer and a high-speed Internet connection. In addition, online learning is often more convenient than traditional face-to-face classes because you can arrange the courses to fit your schedule.

Yet it is not true that online learning is easy. In fact, it would be a mistake to approach any online course with this attitude. Because you aren't sitting in an actual classroom for three hours a week, you may think this is extra time you can use for other things. But online students generally need to use these three hours to log on to course lectures, videos, etc., and take part in online discussions, in addition to the hours they need for study.

There is also the added factor that much of the communication between students and the instructor in online courses takes place through writing. This means that your ability to put your thoughts into words is very important and can be challenging. However, having to write things down can enable you to think carefully about your responses, especially when you do not have to respond instantly. Because online learning gives you a great amount of practice writing, it may have the added benefit of improving your writing skills.

The truth is that online students often find they spend the same amount of time on their online courses as they would have spent for traditional classes. Many online learners actually find online classes are more work than traditional courses they have taken. This is due in part to the amount of reading and writing involved, but it also has to do with the organizational skills and self-discipline necessary to complete course work on time. It would be a mistake to assume that <u>online learning</u> is easier than traditional learning, but after you master the skills necessary to excel at <u>online learning</u>, it can be just as rewarding.

FACT: You Don't Need to Be a Computer Whiz to Take Online Courses

True: It is true that in order to participate in an online course, students should have some computer skills, but it's not necessary to have a great deal of computer experience. If you are comfortable with writing and receiving e-mail and surfing the Web, you probably know enough to get started. It's most important that you have regular access to a computer and high-speed Internet in order to participate in an online course.

Understanding new computer technology can be confusing at times, but this should never be a reason to avoid <u>online learning</u> or to drop out of an online course. Even people who are comfortable with computer technology can become frustrated by new programs. Because online colleges recognize this fact, some provide online computer experts who can help students learn how to use the technology necessary to participate in classes. Some online colleges have help desks available 24/7 that students can call or log on to whenever they need computer support. In addition, many software programs come with instructional CDs or online demos that will walk you through the steps needed to install and use the program.

Don't let worries about technology keep you from starting a class or cause you to drop out later. As part of your research on online providers and courses, it's important to find out the kind of technology support that will be available to you.

MYTH: Online Learning Is Impersonal

False: Another common myth is that online classes will be impersonal and that there will be very little communication between you and the instructor and between you and the other students. However, an <u>online learning</u> environment can be very interactive. Because participants often never meet face to face, they communicate instead through e-mail, <u>instant messaging</u> programs, and discussion groups. Many classes require students to work together on group projects online as well as participate in online discussions and debates.

Today, many online courses also use interactive software programs such as <u>live tutorials,</u> <u>video chats</u>, <u>teleconferencing</u>, and <u>multimedia presentations</u> that allow students and instructors to experience something closer to face-to-face interactions. In some cases, students can see, hear, and respond to instructors as though they were in a classroom.

Not every online course uses interactive programs, but many do, and the technology continues to improve. If online classes with interaction with an instructor and other students are a priority for you, find out if this option is available as part of your research into online providers and courses.

MYTH: Online Learning Is Not as Effective as Traditional Face-to-Face Classroom Learning

False: This is a concern that goes back to when <u>online learning</u> was first being developed in the late 1990s. Many educators insisted that without the face-to-face exchange between instructor and student, <u>online learning</u> could never be as effective as traditional classes. This view has changed greatly over the past decade with the increasing popularity of the personal computer and the public's acceptance of the Internet.

Although online learning is still a relatively new form of education, it has been proven to be a useful way to deliver many different types of information across various fields, whether for a degree, certification, or just a fun way to learn new things. Many universities, colleges, trade associations, and other organizations—not to mention for-profit companies—have embraced online learning as an effective teaching tool and continue to look for new ways to develop the medium. Now the major focus is not on whether online learning is effective, but on how to improve the technology in order to provide instruction in even better ways.

MYTH: Online Classes Are of Lower Quality Than Traditional Classes

False: This may have been true when online learning was first developed and was an unregulated and untested way to deliver educational content. Now, however, any accredited university or college—whether traditional ones that offer online courses or online universities—is regularly audited by its state education department and must meet certain regulations. *Note:* Not all institutions offering online courses are accredited.

Many traditional institutions of higher education and organizations that provide training online have followed the lead of for-profit online universities and have departments devoted solely to developing courses and training instructors in the specific skills necessary to teach online. Because everything is online, including teachers' notes, lectures, test results, and student feedback, it is often easier to check the content of courses and to track teachers' performance. Today, education can be just as rigorous for students taking a course online as it is for those sitting in a traditional classroom.

MYTH: Online Courses Cost Less Than Traditional Classes

Partly True But Mostly False: This may be one of the reasons that so many people are attracted to <u>online learning</u> and in one sense, it *is* true. You will not have to pay for room and board as you would if you were a boarder on a traditional college campus, or for a parking permit, gas, and possibly tolls if you were a commuter. You might also be able to omit student activity fees and other supplemental fees. If you are not pursuing a degree, some classes for fun are offered online for free.

However, in general, tuition for an online course costs about as much as for a traditional class. In some cases, it can cost more if the class is offered at a private university. Fortunately, there are many <u>financial aid</u> opportunities, including federal and state loan programs, for students applying to online schools. In addition, many employers will pay in whole or in part for their employees to earn continuing education credits needed for their jobs. Some employers also have tuition reimbursement programs for employees seeking degrees. It is important to research all your options before you register and pay for an online course or program out of your own pocket.

MYTH: All Online Programs Are the Same

False: It would be hard to find a traditional class or program that is the same from school to school. The same is true for online degree and certification programs. They can vary tremendously and can fall anywhere on a scale from terrible to excellent. It is up to you, the student, to do the research necessary to find the best online courses that will meet your needs.

MYTH: Online Learning Is Mostly for People Who Live Far From Traditional Schools

Partly True But Mostly False: It's true that some people choose online learning because they live far from traditional schools. This was how the concept of distance learning first came about in the late 1800s, and it still applies to some online learners today. It's also true that some people choose an online course because, although they are enrolled in a traditional college, their college does not have a particular course they want to take or schedules it every other year and they need to take it now.

But many people choose online learning for entirely different reasons. For working adults, some of whom may even live close to a college or university, being able to create their own schedules and organize their course work around their jobs and family are factors that draw them to online schools and programs. Today, some students who live on college campuses also sign up for online courses simply because of the convenience. They may also work, or just like the convenience of taking classes sitting on their beds. It is quite possible that in the future, a traditional college education will consist of a balance of face-to-face classes and online course work.

MYTH: It Is Much Easier to Cheat When You're Taking Online Courses

False: Because online education is basically unsupervised, it would be easy to assume that it's easier for students to cheat. For example, how would a professor know that a student's work is really the work of that student? Couldn't students simply cut and paste papers that are available online? If the students can take tests online and the tests aren't supposed to be open book, can the teacher know for sure that students didn't consult their textbooks before answering?

Cheating is a problem for instructors teaching both traditional and online classes, and one they have to deal with. But online courses don't necessarily make it easier to cheat. Many assignments or projects are designed to be specific to each individual student or group. Some teachers work with students from the beginning of the class, helping them create and develop a topic that will be unique to their research. Discussion groups also help teachers get an idea of how students think, allowing the teachers to determine if original work is really being turned in. Some instructors use specialized software that compares each student's paper to the millions of papers available on Internet sites, thus enabling the instructors to determine if the work has been plagiarized.

Cheating while taking online exams isn't easy either. Exams can be made unique for each student. Online tests also can have a timing-out function that makes it difficult for a student to look up all the answers and then write them.

Yet the fact of cheating is a real problem for teachers everywhere. If a student wants to cheat, he or she will find a way, whether online or in a traditional class.

MYTH: Employers Won't Accept Online Degrees

False: In the past, when online learning was still a developing field, many employers may have been wary of online degrees from as-yet untested organizations. But now that millions of students are participating in online learning programs, most employers understand and appreciate the fact that online degrees are just as valid as those from traditional colleges and universities.

It is also important to note that if students earn their degrees online through traditional schools, their diplomas will make no mention of the fact that any or all of their course work was completed online. But as online learning becomes even more commonplace, it is quite possible that some employers may prefer the candidate whose degree was earned online because it may indicate someone with strong writing skills and an ability to manage his or her time well.

MYTH: Online Students Do Not Have the Same Resources Available to Them as Students at Traditional Schools

False: Believe it or not, online students have access to everything available on a traditional college campus. This includes libraries, of course, but it also includes services and programs you might not have considered.

If you have a disability, there are programs that can provide you with the necessary technology and support in order to participate in an online class. Many colleges offer their students programs such as internship placement, career services, and research and study facilities. All of these are available not only to students living on or commuting to campus, but also to those logging on from home. Before you sign up for an online class, find out what else you might be able to take advantage of in order to enrich your educational experience.

COMMON MISTAKES ONLINE LEARNERS MAKE

One important truth about online learning is that there tends to be a high dropout rate. Students either quit a class halfway through or drop out of a program after taking one or two courses. This problem stems from many of the misconceptions we have already covered about online learning, but dropping out can also be a result of mistakes that online learners tend to make when they are first starting out. If you become familiar with some of the most common mistakes of first-time online learners, hopefully you will be able to avoid them!

Not Researching the School

Choosing the right school for an online course or program may be the most important challenge you face. If you are earning a degree or need certification or continuing education credits (CEUs), it is important to find an online school that is <u>accredited</u> so that other schools and employers will accept the credits you earn. You can find out if an institution is <u>accredited</u> by looking at the U.S. Department of Education's Web site (http://www.ope.ed.gov/accreditation/) or the Web site of the Council of Higher Education Accreditation (www.chea.org). Both Web sites list thousands of <u>accredited</u> colleges and universities. You should also be careful to avoid "<u>diploma mills,</u>" which are known for charging students thousands of dollars for degrees that are worthless.

You can do much of your research online, but you might also check with co-workers or your employer to find out which online colleges they have had good experiences with and can recommend. In addition to finding out if a school is <u>accredited</u>, you should do research to find out which types of resources and support are provided. If you have a learning or physical disability, find out if there are resources that will help you succeed in an online course. If you need help with your computer skills, find out if the school or organization offers online tech support. Before you make a commitment to any online course or program, it's important to do your homework!

Not Managing Time

Even though online students save time by not having to commute or sit in classes, they tend to spend more time reading and studying. It is important to consider just how much time you will really need before you sign up for an online course. Many students find they need to spend up to fifteen to twenty hours a week on each class. Because your time can be much more flexible with online learning, these hours can be broken up into small chunks—except for those hours you spend in a synchronous class. Regardless of the type of course you take, be prepared to put in a similar number of hours a week.

It can be helpful to develop a routine in which you always study at a certain time each day. This way, you will be able to fit in the required number of hours each week for studying. It can also be helpful to sign up for just one course when you begin online learning so you do not become overwhelmed. Once you get a sense of how much time you really have available for your online program, you can add courses as needed.

Not Considering Learning Style

Think about how you learn best:

- Can you handle a lot of reading material?

- Can you work mostly by yourself or does this make you feel isolated?

- Do you like to have a large amount of social interaction with your classmates?

- Can you set up a schedule for getting your work done and follow it without supervision?

Online learning is probably best for those students who are self-disciplined, able to set their own deadlines and stick to them, who can absorb most of their information by reading, and who feel comfortable expressing their thoughts in writing. If this does not describe you, then online learning might not be the best choice for you. It is important to know exactly what you are getting into before you make your decision.

Not Making Sure the Right Technology Is Available

You don't need to be a computer expert, but you do need to have regular access to a computer and you also need a high-speed Internet connection. You might also need to have some basic software, such as Microsoft Word or Excel, which many online schools require for turning in written work. Anything less than the basic requirements will make it extremely difficult to get your assignments completed on time and will seriously hinder your online experience.

Not Being Organized

Many online students also have full-time jobs and family obligations. This is why being organized is extremely important. Because you can complete your online course work at your own pace, there is a tendency to put off doing the work until it is too late. Many students end up dropping out because they cannot get their course work done on time.

One way to solve this problem is to organize both your time and your course materials. You can set up an organized system on your computer to keep track of your assignments, your e-mail, and other online correspondence. Your study area should be organized as well, so that you can always find what you are looking for when you need it.

Not Being Motivated

It would be easy to think that just because you can do <u>online learning</u> at your own pace, you don't have to work as hard as you might in a traditional college or program. Yet if you are not motivated enough to study or if you simply keep putting it off, you will likely fall behind and will be more likely to drop out as a result. You should approach any <u>online learning</u> experience as seriously as you would any other educational or work experience in your life.

Not Having a Proper Place to Study

When you are ready to study, it is important to have a place that is both quiet and comfortable and where you can focus on your work for as long as necessary without being distracted. In an ideal world, you would have an office with a door you could close in order to get all your online course work completed. Most people do not have this option, of course, and many parents find that the only time they can study is after their children go to bed.

If you find yourself studying in a distracting place with too much noise or activity, you will be very unlikely to get any work done. Even before you consider taking an online class, you should determine if you will have a proper place to log on and to study.

Not Having Support

<u>Online learning</u> can make demands on your life that are challenging, but it will be even more challenging if you do not have support from your family and friends. If you work at a full-time job, it is likely that you will be working on your online course work during the evenings or weekends, when your family and friends are most likely to want your attention. If they do not understand or support your efforts at <u>online learning</u>, it will be very difficult to get anything accomplished.

Not Being Willing to Interact or Cooperate with Other Students Online

Many online courses require students to interact with other students in the class and to work on group projects. This is part of the online learning experience, and it is important to stay connected with the other students in your class through e-mail, message boards, or chat rooms. Often these relationships can help you to learn more through an exchange of ideas and can help you stay motivated. It is also important to cooperate when you are working on group projects. Working well in a group is a skill that many employers look for, and neglecting this part of your online experience would be a mistake.

Networking is another important benefit of online group interactions. You may be able to form relationships with students and instructors who can help you once you graduate. If you think someone can assist you in the future, be sure to give that person your contact information and to get theirs before the course is over.

Not Researching How to Pay for Online Learning

All schools, traditional or online, cost money—and sometimes more than you might have expected. However, there are many opportunities for online students to receive financial aid, such as scholarships, grants, and loans. Many companies will pay all or part of the tuition for their employees to earn continuing education credits or a job-related degree online. In addition, books, computer software, and other supplies needed for your courses can often be found online at lower prices. You might also be able to find free research help and online books that can help you with your course work. All it takes is some research.

Not Getting Credit for Previous Course work at Other Schools

If you have taken courses and gotten credit for them from other schools, you may be able to get some or all of the credit applied to your online degree. You will need to check with your online school first and you will likely have to get your transcripts from previous school(s) sent to your current online school. Occasionally, you may be allowed to receive credit for work or even life experience. It never hurts to check! All these efforts can save you money.

 WILL AN ONLINE LEARNING PROGRAM WORK FOR YOU? QUIZ

It's time to take an honest look at how your expectations and learning style—how you learn—match with the reality of online learning programs. Complete the following quiz and find out if you and online learning are in synch.

1. The amount of time I expect to spend on online course work is

   A. more than a traditional course.

   B. the same as a traditional course.

   C. less than a traditional course.

2. My reading skills are

   A. very good. I usually understand things the first time I read them.

   B. average. Sometimes I need to go over sections a few times for clarification and I sometimes need help from an instructor to understand the material.

   C. not great. I have to reread many sections and usually need help from an instructor to understand the material.

3. When it comes to deadlines for assignments,

   A. I usually have assignments completed ahead of time.

   B. I usually have assignments completed on time, but sometimes need reminders about deadlines.

   C. I forget assignments are due if I'm not reminded regularly.

4. When given a new assignment, I prefer to

   A. figure out the instructions on my own.

   B. try to understand the instructions, and then ask for further clarification if needed.

   C. have the instructions explained to me in detail.

5. I prefer my feedback from an instructor to be

   A. written comments.

   B. written comments with some oral clarifications if needed.

   C. oral comments.

6. Classroom discussion is

   A. very important to how I learn.

   B. somewhat important to how I learn.

   C. not important to how I learn.

7. I learn best

   A. by reading using visual aids, such as charts and diagrams (visual learning style).

   B. when someone explains things to me orally (auditory).

   C. by doing hands-on work myself such as a lab experiment (kinesthetic).

8. Having face-to-face contact with my instructors is

   A. not important to me.

   B. somewhat important to me.

   C. very important to me.

9. The socialization part of the traditional on-campus experience is

   A. not very important to me.

   B. somewhat important to me.

   C. very important to me.

10. The main reason I am considering taking an online class is because

   A. I really enjoy using the Internet, and this seems like a good way to take a class.

   B. the class I need is only available online.

   C. I want to save time.

If your answers consist mostly of A's:

Online learning would likely work well for you and your learning style. However, you still need to figure out how to incorporate your online classes into your lifestyle.

If your answers consist mostly of B's:

Online learning can work for you, but you may need to make some adjustments to your learning style in order to have a satisfying experience.

If your answers consist mostly of C's:

You may want to think about whether an online class is right for you. You could find it an unsatisfying or disappointing experience unless you made some major changes to what you expect from a class situation and how you are most comfortable processing information, interacting with an instructor and fellow students, and completing assignments.

SAMPLE ONLINE COURSE EVALUATION FORM

Sometimes students are asked to fill out an evaluation form after completing an online course. In this way, the providers of the course get feedback from students to better prepare their courses in the future. Here is a sample evaluation form that was adapted from one created by StudentAffairs.com for an online course.

1. On a scale of 1–5, with 1 being NOT AT ALL PREPARED and 5 being VERY PREPARED, how prepared did you feel to participate in an online course?

1   2   3   4   5

2. How much time did you EXPECT to spend on this course?

   1-2 hours/week   3-4 hours/week   5-6 hours/week

   7-8 hours/week   9+ hours/week

3. How much time did you ACTUALLY spend on this course?

   less than 1 hr/week   1-2 hours/week   3-4 hours/week

   5-6 hours/week   7+/week

4. The amount of independent work in this course was

   too little   just about right   too much

5. The amount of reading given in this course was

   too little   just about right   too much

6. On a scale of 1-5, with 5 being the best, do you feel your expectations for this course were met?

   1   2   3   4   5

7. On a scale of 1-5, with 5 being the best, how responsive was the instructor during the course?

   1   2   3   4   5

8. How much direct feedback/input did you EXPECT from the instructor?

   daily   few times a week   weekly   none

9. On a scale of 1–5, with 5 being very satisfied, how satisfied were you with the course format?

1   2   3   4   5

10. On a scale of 1–5, with 5 being the highest, what would be your overall rating for this course?

1   2   3   4   5

11. Do you feel the price for this course was

low   just right   too high

12. Do you feel the number of weeks for this course was

not long enough   just right   too long

13. Was this your first online course?   Yes   No

14. Would you take another online course?   Yes   No

15. Why? Why not?

16. Would you recommend an online course to a friend or colleague?   Yes   No

17. What did you like best about the course?

18. What are some improvements or changes that could improve the course?

TRYING OUT ONLINE LEARNING FOR FREE

If you're still undecided about <u>online learning</u>, you may be able to get a sense of what it's like by taking a course online for free. There are two readily available options: OpenCourseWare and free online courses.

You won't get any credit for taking these courses, and you won't have access to instructors or other students, but you will get a good idea of what online courses are like. Some are very much like real courses in that they include audio lectures, videos, interactive quizzes, and self-directed assignments. Most of these classes include reading lists, which will involve some online research in order to find the best deals.

OpenCourseWare

With OpenCourseWare, colleges and universities make available online free materials from actual courses, including readings, assignments, syllabi, and lecture notes. These courses might also provide access to free online videos and lectures used in the course. Students around the world use OpenCourseWare to sample college courses online.

To begin learning with OpenCourseWare, you simply need to go to a school's Web site, scroll through the list of available courses and lectures, make your selection, and then download them. You might need to acquire some new software programs, including a <u>media player</u>, to take full advantage of all course materials, but these will likely be available free online. A few schools require you to register for OpenCourseWare using your e-mail address, but most do not ask for registration.

The following is a list of some of the best OpenCourseWare programs available online:

- MIT was the first college to offer OpenCourseWare and its offerings have grown to over 1,000 free online courses, which are available in plain text and audio and video formats; many have been translated into other languages. http://ocw.mit.edu/OcwWeb/web/home/home/index.htm

- Tufts University provides students with access to course materials from a number of fields, including medicine, nutrition, and the arts. The courses are arranged by school, such as the School of Arts and Sciences or the School of Medicine. http://ocw.tufts.edu

- The Fulbright Economics Teaching Program offers OpenCourseWare programs in economics and public policy. Many courses are available online and the school plans to eventually include all Fulbright School course materials on its Web site. http://ocw.fetp.edu.vn/home.cfm

- The Johns Hopkins Bloomberg School of Public Health offers many health-related courses. http://ocw.jhsph.edu

- Carnegie Mellon University offers a number of free online courses and materials through its Open Learning Initiative. These courses in a variety of subjects are actually designed for online learners and include all the materials you will need. http://oli.web.cmu.edu/openlearning/forstudents

- The University of California, Irvine, was the first West Coast university to offer OpenCourseWare. Its online course materials are available in various subjects and are targeted for working adults who, after trying out some free courses, might consider enrolling in for-credit courses. http://ocw.uci.edu

- Utah State University provides access to dozens of free online courses that can be downloaded as zip files or viewed directly on the site. http://ocw.usu.edu

While the following offerings are outside of the OpenCourseWare structure, they offer free learning programs online:

- Stanford University has made many of its courses, lectures, and interviews available through iTunes. These courses can be downloaded and played on PCs, Macs, and iPods and can also be burned onto CDs, all for free. http://itunes.stanford.edu

- Kutztown University Small Business Development Center offers one of the largest collections of free business courses, including accounting, finance, government, business law, and marketing, available on the Web. The site asks its participants to register, but membership is free. http://www.kutztownsbdc.org/course_listing.asp

Free Online Courses

Another option is the thousands of free online classes available on the Web. Not all are of the same quality, so it will take some research online to find the best free class to suit your purpose. It's helpful to begin with a subject that interests you or a topic that will help you professionally and then begin a search for some online courses. If your goal is to find out if online learning will work for you, you should try to choose an online course that has a workload and schedule similar to that of a for-credit course.

Here is just a small sample of some free online course offerings:

- The Online Education Database provides a list of 200 free online classes on various Web sites that cover topics in science, math, computer science, health, law, history, theology, business and finance, and a number of other areas.
www.oedb.org/library/beginning-online-learning/200-free-online-classes-to-learn-anything

- The Small Business Administration provides links to free multimedia courses that teach you how to plan and run a small business.
http://www.sba.gov/index.html

- Poynter's News University provides online courses in journalism and media training. The courses are in the form of tutorials, Webinars, online seminars, and self-directed courses.
www.newsu.org

- Rutgers, The State University of New Jersey, offers multimedia online courses in Chinese that supplement Chinese courses offered at universities.
http://chinese.rutgers.edu

- The BBC (British Broadcasting Company) offers a number of online courses in a variety of subjects (www.bbc.co.uk/learning/onlinecourses) and also free online courses and training in broadcast media (www.bbctraining.com/onlineCourses.asp)

- Web sites like Open Culture (www.openculture.com/freeonlinecourses) and Academic Earth (http://academicearth.org) have compiled links to hundreds of free online courses offered by universities around the world. The courses are listed by academic subject.

Practice Run

To get the full experience while taking a free online or OpenCourseWare class, you should approach it as though it were for credit. If the class offers a suggested schedule, try to stick to it or set up a schedule for yourself and try to meet your own deadlines. You should also complete assignments with the expectation that your work will be graded.

Once you have completed the course, ask yourself if you enjoyed the experience and if it met your expectations. Although a real online learning program won't be exactly the same, you will have a good idea if this is something you want to pursue.

▶ COMMON MISTAKES YOU WON'T MAKE CHECKLIST

The following are the things you need to do so you won't make the mistakes people make who are unprepared for what online learning requires.

- ☐ Consider if online learning is right for me.
- ☐ Do research to identify potential schools.
- ☐ Do research and decide how to pay for my online courses.
- ☐ Find out if my credits from previous schools can be applied to my current program.
- ☐ Complete the necessary work to have credits forwarded and applied to my current program.
- ☐ Figure out before I start my course how to manage my time.
- ☐ Make a proper place to study.
- ☐ Make sure I have the right technology.
- ☐ Organize my course materials at the beginning of the course.
- ☐ Figure out ways to stay motivated throughout the course.

☐ Explain to my family and friends before the course starts why I am taking the course and ask for their help and support.

☐ Once I start the course, interact and cooperate with other students online to participate in group work.

Degrees, Certificates, Lifelong Learning: Programs for All Kinds of Needs

• •

"In my online courses, I still try to practice what I once preached to my teacher education students in the classroom. That is, let the students know what to expect from the course, let them know what to expect from you, and let them know what you expect of them. I believe this is best for all types of instruction, not just classroom instruction and not just academic credit instruction. Also, this needs to be done up front and early on in the course."

Mark A. Davenport, PhD
Senior Research Analyst
Office of Institutional Research
The University of North Carolina at Greensboro

• •

There are all kinds of online programs available, depending on what you are looking for. Do you want to finish college and earn a degree—associate or bachelor's? Are you interested in earning a graduate degree? Are you looking to demonstrate your competency in a job by earning certification in it? Do you need continuing education credits for your career? Or are you simply interested in taking a class to learn something new? This chapter describes the variety of options available online.

ONLINE DEGREE AND CERTIFICATE PROGRAMS

Online degree programs are convenient and flexible for most working adults, allowing them to complete a degree at their own pace, whether part-time or full-time. It is possible to get associate's degrees, bachelor's degrees, and graduate degrees, both master's and doctorates. Online colleges and universities as well as some traditional colleges and universities offer degrees online. There are many options for earning online degree.

Online Associate Degree

. . . .

"In 2002, my oldest child enrolled at Hudson Valley [Community College], and because I wanted to advance in my career, I decided to enroll there, too. I started classes when I was working three days a week, but after a couple of years, I was working full-time and taking two to three courses a semester... There's no way I would have finished this degree without online courses. With three children and my job, there was no way I could come to campus and complete a degree... I'm so grateful that the school offered this option."

Sue Jones
Associate of Arts, Individual Studies, 2006
Hudson Valley Community College

. . . .

An associate degree is an academic degree usually awarded by community and junior colleges or technical institutes, though some four-year colleges and universities also offer two-year associate degree programs. The two most common associate degrees are an Associate of Arts (AA), for degrees in the humanities or social sciences, and an Associate of Science (AS), for degrees in mathematics, life science, physical science, or technology. Some schools also confer Associate in Applied Arts (AAA) and Associate in Applied Science (AAS) degrees. Most associate degree programs require 60 credits to graduate and take two years to complete if students enroll as full-time students.

Associate degrees are available in a variety of fields, including business, information technology, communications, engineering, marketing, and health care. Some people choose to earn an associate degree in order to become more qualified in their fields or to earn a degree quickly so they can enter the work force sooner. Employees with an associate degree generally earn more than those who have only a high school diploma or GED.

Some people choose to start with an associate degree as a cost-saving measure because community colleges typically cost less than four-year institutions, even public in-state schools. At the end of the two years with associate degree in hand, they transfer to a four-year college where they earn 60 more credits for a bachelor's degree.

There are also associate degrees known as career or professional associate degrees that can qualify you for certain entry-level positions in fields that do not require a bachelor's degree, such as medical assisting, computer programming, criminal justice, and paralegal studies. However, credits from this type of associate's degree may not be transferable to a bachelor's degree program.

Online Bachelor's Degree

. . . .

**"I took a linguistics course during the summer because it
was offered online and I already had a rigorous course
schedule so I didn't want the confines of an actual
classroom. We had daily homework that we used our
textbook for, and we had timed tests that became
available at a certain time, which we had to complete
within an hour and a half. We had to log on every day to
do the homework and be a part of the discussion board. If
we had any questions, we could always post to the
message board and have a discussion about it. The
course lasted six weeks, just as long as my other summer
classes, and I really loved it."**

Karen Goldfarb
BS, Psychobiology, 2007
Binghamton University, State University of New York

. . . .

A bachelor's degree from an undergraduate college or university
usually takes four years full-time to complete and requires 120
credits. More than half the credits toward a bachelor's degree
usually consist of general courses in subjects such as English,
psychology, history, a foreign language, and mathematics. Another
thirty to 36 credits will be in the major area of study. Students who
participate in a bachelor's degree program usually need to declare a
major by the end of their second year.

Students can complete online bachelor's degree programs in a
wide variety of subjects. The two most common bachelor's degrees
are the Bachelor of Arts (BA), for degrees in the humanities, arts,
and social sciences, and the Bachelor of Science (BS or BSc), for
degrees in the life, earth, and physical sciences and mathematics.
Many professional careers require a bachelor's degree. Graduate

schools in the fields of law, medicine, and teacher education do not admit students without bachelor's degrees.

Online Master's Degree

. . . .

"I got my MBA online because it was the only way I had a chance to complete a degree. My job involved constant travel so there was no way I could sit in a classroom. A few times I had tried working on a degree in a traditional classroom setting, but I always ended up having to drop out due to attendance."

Marion Waldman
Master of Business Administration, 2006
University of Maryland University College

. . . .

Online master's degree programs generally take about two to three years to complete, not unlike traditional master's degree programs. However, some online master's degree programs are set up so that students can take one course at a time, starting each new course right after the last one is completed. Course lengths also tend to be compressed. Most master's degree programs require students to complete a master's thesis, or an extended research paper, though some programs offer alternatives to the master's thesis, such as a written comprehensive exam.

The most common types of master's degrees are Master of Arts (MA), Master of Science (MS), and Master of Business Administration (MBA), which is a graduate degree in business, usually with a particular focus such as finance, marketing, or technology. There are also a number of specialized master's degrees, including Master of Fine Arts (MFA), Master of Social

Work (MSW), Master of Education (MEd), Master of Engineering (MEng), Master of Public Health (MPH), and Master of Science in Nursing (MSN).

Many students earn master's degrees to advance in their careers and to earn more money. A master's degree can also allow a person to begin a new career. For instance, a person with a bachelor's degree in English who decides to become a teacher could earn a Master of Arts in Teaching (MAT) or a Master of Education (MEd). A master's degree is also a necessary prerequisite for a doctoral degree.

Today, many employers looking to fill management positions in fields such as sales and marketing, information technology, engineering, and finance seek candidates with master's degrees. A master's degree is usually a requirement for most teachers in public schools—after a certain number of years, if not for initial employment—and for postsecondary teaching positions.

Online Doctoral Degree

. . . .

"I always wanted to get my doctorate in pharmacy. It was not a job requirement to have a PharmD but I knew that I was capable of doing the work and obtaining the degree. . . I researched several pharmacy schools and the one that I chose had the easiest format. . . The course work was solely online and the rotations afterward were tailored to the working pharmacist with a family. I think that taking an online course requires a tremendous amount of dedication to complete all the work on time. It was a challenge to find the time after working all day and then taking care of the kids to then sit down to do school work."

Dario Pantano
Doctor of Pharmacy (PharmD), 2010
University of Colorado

. . . .

A doctoral degree is the highest academic degree you can earn. The most common doctoral degree is the Doctor of Philosophy (PhD), which can be awarded in many fields, from philosophy to English to history to chemistry. Other doctoral degrees include the Doctor of Education (EdD), Doctor of Engineering (EngD), Doctor of Pharmacy (PharmD), and Doctor of Psychology (PsyD). A traditional doctoral program usually requires four to ten years of additional study beyond the master's degree. (Some doctoral programs include a master's degree as part of it.) However, many online doctoral programs may take only two to four years of full-time study.

You might be surprised to learn that you can receive a doctoral degree online, but as the need has grown, an increasing number of schools are making doctoral programs available online.

To receive a doctoral degree, students must complete advanced courses in a chosen field, do original research, and write a <u>thesis</u> or <u>dissertation,</u> which is submitted for publication. Doctoral work generally involves a great deal of independent research, which makes it an appropriate degree to earn online.

Online Certification

. . . .

"Although I already had an MS in education and held two New York State teaching certificates, I was having a difficult time finding employment as an elementary teacher. I decided to take the twelve credits necessary that would allow me to transition into the field of special education. . . I took fully accredited master's level courses in eight-week cycles, rather than the typical twelve- to sixteen-week semester. This accelerated program allowed me to finish my course work and apply for my NYS certification in a reduced time period."

Marni Tesser
MS, Elementary Education, 1995
Hunter College
Nonmatriculated Student of Special Education, 2009
Grand Canyon University

. . . .

Certification programs provide students with a wide array of professional opportunities. Individuals may enroll in certification programs to qualify for entry-level positions in certain fields, to learn specific skills, or to advance in their fields. For example, there are many new occupations emerging from the green energy sector of the economy such as solar panel installer and automotive technician for hybrid cars. To help individuals qualify for clean-tech jobs, trade associations, technical schools, and community colleges are developing short-course online training programs.

Another reason to enroll in certification programs is to demonstrate to prospective employers that you have the necessary skills and competency for a particular job. For example, if you currently have a bachelor's degree in computer science, earning a specific certificate, such as an Apple Certified System Administrator or Certified Information Systems Auditor, may improve your chances of landing the job you want now—and promotions in the future.

In education, certificate programs are designed for teachers who want to enhance their skills or to focus on a new specialty such as curriculum development, literacy, instructional technology, administration, or special education. These programs may also help teachers satisfy their requirements for continuing education units necessary for retaining their teaching licenses.

Online certificate programs are more focused than degree programs, meaning they can often be completed over several weeks or months.

CONTINUING EDUCATION ONLINE

. . . .

"In order to remain licensed in Pennsylvania, attorneys must complete twelve continuing legal education credits each year. An attorney may complete any course as long as it comes from an accredited agency and is recognized and approved by our bar association. . . We are currently permitted to take four of our credits through an online class. It's an easy and convenient way to fulfill our credits, and it permits us to do it when it suits our schedules. I'm able to complete the classes at night or on the weekends. . . I can even pause a lecture if necessary and resume it when I'm ready to continue. Hopefully, we will be able to complete more credits online at some time in the future."

Deborah Ryan, Esq.
Assistant District Attorney
Chester County District Attorney's Office

. . . .

Typically, professionals who hold licenses to practice such as doctors and teachers must take a certain number of continuing education credits to maintain their licenses. Depending on the profession, the credits must be taken annually or within a certain number of years on a regular cycle, such as every two years or every three years. These professionals include architects, engineers, educators, nurses, mental health professionals, lawyers, real estate agents, and social workers. The purpose of the course work is to ensure that professionals remain up-to-date on new developments in their fields.

Instead of using college credits, many continuing education programs use continuing education units (CEU), which is a nationally recognized system of recording participation in professional continuing education programs. (Legal units are called LEUs [legal education units].) One CEU is defined as "ten contact hours of participation in an organized continuing education experience under responsible sponsorship, capable direction, and qualified instruction." Responsible sponsorship refers to an accredited educational institution, which is important information to check when researching any online learning program in which you are thinking about enrolling.

Typically with online continuing education programs, you may choose from a variety of topics in your field. You complete reading assignments and take tests at your own pace to fulfill the credit hours you need.

 ## SAMPLE COURSE OVERVIEW AND SYLLABUS

The following is the course overview and syllabus for a continuing education class in SSPS, a computer program used for statistical analysis. The course is taught by Mark A. Davenport at The University of North Carolina at Greensboro. The overview gives you an idea of how his course is organized and what he expects of his online students. The syllabus shows how the course is set up on Blackboard, a software program used by many schools for online courses.

A STUDENT AFFAIRS PROFESSIONAL'S GUIDE TO DATA REPORTING USING SPSS FOR WINDOWS

Course Overview

Higher education is data intensive, and the student personnel area of higher education is certainly no exception. This course is designed to give student affairs professionals knowledge and practical experience using SPSS to answer assessment-related

and evaluation-related questions. NO PRIOR SPSS OR STATISTI-
CAL EXPERIENCE IS REQUIRED!

Using your own data or a dataset provided by the instructor,
you will:

- Learn to create SPSS data files from scratch or from
  existing data in other formats.

- Add and change variables.

- Create charts and tables.

- Learn how to create charts and graphs that are accurate
  and easy to interpret.

- Use charts, tables, and descriptive statistics to address
  questions common to student personnel work.

Although this course will be tailored to SPSS software, it is NOT
strictly a "how to" course on the use of SPSS. You will also be
learning the best practices of statistical reporting.

Also be advised that this is NOT a course on statistical
inference. We will be using only descriptive statistics such as
means, frequencies, and cross-tabulation tables as these are the
primary tools of the student affairs professional.

Course Outline

Although I will have a dataset available and will be teaching
from that dataset, this course will be much more useful and
meaningful if you have a dataset of your own. We will begin the
course by developing research questions that we wish to answer
with our data. As research is often a social enterprise, we will be
sharing our ideas via Web discussion with the other course
participants. We will read your data into SPSS from whatever
format you are using. I will provide instruction on importing data
from a variety of sources including Excel, ACCESS, OBDC,
flat-file data (tab-, comma-, column-delimited) using the Text
Import Wizard, etc.

We will examine ways to describe data using frequency counts, percentages, and, when appropriate, measures of central tendency such as the mean. You will learn which description methods are most appropriate for particular forms of data, how to create new variables such as sum scores and means, how to identify bad data, and how to deal with problems such as outliers and missing data.

Once you have practiced your data manipulation skills, we will address accepted best practices in statistical reporting and you will learn how to create tables, charts, and graphs that communicate your message efficiently and effectively.

In the course of learning SPSS, we will use the menu system to do much of the work. However, you will also learn how to take advantage of SPSS syntax and simple macros to create short-cuts that could save you hours of "pointing and clicking." If you come into this course with a real dataset and real questions, you should finish with report-ready tables and charts.

In sum, upon completion of this course, you should be able to:

- Recognize the advantage of using statistical software in student personnel work.

- Create, manipulate, and process simple datasets using SPSS.

- Create simple tables and charts using SPSS.

- Follow accepted best practices in statistical reporting.

- Understand why simple spreadsheets such as Excel are woefully inadequate for statistical reporting.

Required Resources

You must have access to a PC with the SPSS for Windows Base Module (any version from 14 to 18) installed. Your institution likely has a site license that will allow you to use SPSS from the network or from a CD. Please install the software and make sure it is running properly *before* you register for this course.

Optional Resources

Most any beginner's guide to SPSS will be helpful. A separate statistics book is not necessary, but I will provide a list of books, articles, and Web sites that I consider good, basic references for descriptive statistics and graphics.

Syllabus

Course Day 1: Wednesday, June 24

Introduction to SPSS

Readings:

The history of SPSS:

http://www.spss.com/corpinfo/history.htm

Why use SPSS rather than, say Excel?:

http://www.ag.unr.edu/gf/apst650/excelprob1.pdf

Course Day 2: Friday, June 26

First steps: Entering data, importing data.

The Data View Window

The Variable View Window

Readings:

Levels of Measurement:

http://www.socialresearchmethods.net/kb/measlevl.htm

http://en.wikipedia.org/wiki/Level_of_measurement

Course Day 3: Monday, June 29

Second steps: Importing data

Drawing in data from a flat file, Excel, and via
    database query

The magic of syntax

Course Day 4: Wednesday, July 1

Learning to run: Using syntax and practicing with
    syntax

Course Day 5: Friday, July 3

Learning to fly: Syntax for COMPUTE and RECODE

Creating variables and changing them

Course Day 6: Monday, July 6
Merging and aggregating datasets

Course Day 7: Wednesday, July 8
Data analysis: Frequencies, Crosstabs, Descriptive statistics

Course Day 8: Friday, July 10
Creating and using filter variables; Descriptives

Course Day 9: Monday, July 13
Just showing off: Creating Charts using SPSS

ONLINE LEARNING FOR FUN

. . . .

"I took an online writing class called 'Manuscript Review for Children's Writers.' The class is led by a teacher, and has about twelve students. Every week you post up to 2,500 words, and receive critiques from two other students as well as the teacher. . . I had been dreaming about getting an MFA in writing, but spending the money on tuition was not an option. Also, as an at-home mom I needed to figure out something that worked with my children's schedules, so an online class was perfect. . . This class has been a phenomenal experience for me. I have benefited tremendously from the extensive and engaged feedback I've received."

Robyn Pforr Ryan
Online writing class at www.writers.com

. . . .

If you are a lifelong learner, online classes can be a really fun way to continue your intellectual search. There are probably more subjects available for <u>online learning</u> than there are words in this chapter. Here, for example, is a random sample of the offerings from a single Web site that specializes in online courses:

English Composition

Blogging Basics

Introduction to the Internet

Acrylic Bird Painting

Photojournalism and
    Documentary Photography

Medicinal Herbs

Personal Finance

Understanding Child
    Development

Business and Management
    Introduction

Photoshop 3D

The Art of Collage with Corel
    Painter

There are hundreds more such courses. Go to any search engine, type in a subject that interests you—whether it's travel, U.S. history, organic gardening, or digital photography—and find an online course that teaches it. You might, for example, find a course that consists of <u>video lectures</u> of a university professor's chapter-by-chapter reading of a classic novel. You might also find an online <u>tutorial</u> showing you how to paint with watercolors. After creating your own paintings, you would send in digital photos of your work and receive feedback from the instructor online.

Many online classes are led by instructors, with lessons posted over the course of a certain number of weeks. Assignments must be completed by a certain date. Another option for <u>online learning</u> is called a <u>self-study</u> class. This kind of online class costs less because there is no instructor feedback or class <u>message board</u>. However, once you enroll, all the lessons and materials are available to be downloaded and you can work at your own pace for as long as it takes to complete the course.

ONLINE LEARNING FOR HIGH SCHOOL STUDENTS

<u>Online learning</u> isn't just for those in college or in the work force. According to the Sloan Consortium, an organization that researches and supports <u>online learning</u>, the number of K–12 students in U.S. public schools who took online courses in 2007–2008 was estimated at 1,030,000, which represented a 47 percent increase over the 700,000 students enrolled in 2005–2006.

<u>Online learning</u> can be a powerful tool for students who want to take more advanced courses not offered in their own schools. These include specialized language programs, such as Basic Mandarin, and Advanced Placement (AP), challenging courses that are taught in high school but on a college level. Because some schools don't have the resources to offer AP courses in subjects such as U.S. Government and Politics,

Calculus BC, and Latin, online programs can bring these classes to students in schools in any part of the country.

Virtual High School (www.govhs.org) has been offering online AP and electives to high schools in thirty states and thirty-four countries since 1996. Some of the courses offered by VHS include AP classes in biology, economics, and Spanish, as well as such elective offerings as American Popular Music and Great Inventions and Scientific Discoveries. The wide variety of VHS courses would not ordinarily be available in typical schools. To participate in the VHS program, a school must agree to have at least one teacher from that school teach a VHS online course as part of his or her normal teaching responsibility.

There are also online high schools offering AP courses to students who can't fit their own high school's offerings into their schedules. For example, Indiana University High School (www.iuhighschool.iu.edu) is a fully accredited online high school that offers AP classes in English, math, and social studies. The courses are available in a self-paced format for twelve months or can be taken by semester for four months at a time.

Familiarity with online courses in high school can be very helpful once students reach college. The Sloan Consortium reports that in 2004, there were 2.5 million college students taking at least one course online. This was 11 percent of matriculated students, and the number is estimated to grow at the rate of 400,000 students a year.

High school students who are struggling can also find help online. They can participate in online programs over the summer so they can catch up with their classmates. Some school districts are using online course systems for summer school. Students log on and take intensive course work that covers a semester's worth of material in four weeks.

Chapter 4 `Go`

Choosing an Online School

. . . .

"My program is relatively new and is only beginning to earn state-by-state accreditation. As such, there are very few schools that offer it. There is only one traditional school within a 50-mile radius of my house that offers the program, but it was too expensive. I took a look at online schools and concluded that if I were going to be doing schoolwork at night, at least I could do it in the comfort of my own home."

Joe Rosenfeld
MS, Mental Health Counseling, 2013
Walden University

. . . .

. . . .

"I decided to go back to school and get an MBA. There is no local program available in Helena, Montana, where I live, so going with a distance learning program was really the only option. Accreditation, cost, and distance were the major factors in deciding which program to choose. None of the programs I researched were purely online MBA programs, or, if they were, they were not accredited. All the programs had some component of travel, at least a few times per year. The University of Montana in Missoula was the only program that was cost-effective in regard to both the travel requirements and tuition."

Dennis Wizeman
MBA, 2012
University of Montana

. . . .

Once you have decided to take an online course for credit or to pursue an online degree, it's time to do your homework. When there are thousands online to choose from, how do you know which is the right course or program and school for you?

RESEARCHING ONLINE SCHOOLS

The only way to find out is to do as much research as you can. Students spend a great deal of time finding out everything they can about traditional colleges and universities, so there's no reason not to spend as much time researching online institutions. Just as there are a variety of traditional colleges out there, there are many different types of online schools with different qualifications, offerings, instructors, and expectations.

Number 1 Question: Accreditation

The most important question to ask as you research online degree programs is whether the entity offering the program is <u>accredited</u>. Accreditation means that it's recognized as a legitimate educational institution. If your online school is not properly <u>accredited</u>, your degree may be worthless. You face rejection by other schools if you wish to transfer or by prospective employers. We will take a closer look at accreditation in the next section.

Information You Need to Research

As you begin to research your online school, check www.petersons.com/college-search/distance-education.aspx for ideas (as seen on the next page). You can search by course of study, degree/award level, and on-campus requirements. If you have a particular school in mind, you can also search by entering the name of the college or university.

You can also check the rankings of online universities on the Internet. One good site to explore is the Online Education Database (oedb.org/rankings), which clearly explains the criteria it uses to determine its rankings of online schools.

Once you've selected some potential schools, check out their Web sites for further information about courses and degree programs offered online.

- Download any relevant brochures. Some schools may also mail brochures or information packets.

- Read the schools' <u>message boards</u> to see what current and past students have to say about the online programs.

- See if there are any blogs about the school and its programs.

- Ask friends or relatives if they've ever heard of the schools you are considering and what their experiences have been.

Here is a list of questions to ask as you do your homework about online schools:

- **What degrees are offered online?** Not every online program offers every kind of degree. Before you enroll, make sure that your school offers the degree program you want to pursue, whether an associate's degree, bachelor's degree, or graduate degree.

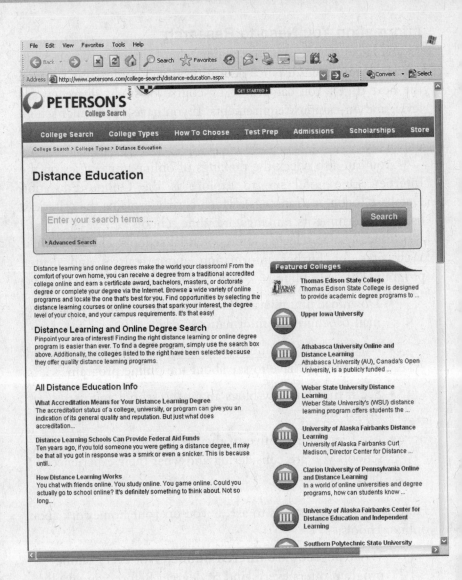

- **What's the tuition?** Your tuition should be about the same as what tuition costs in traditional colleges and universities. It might be slightly less, however, because there are certain on-campus fees you may not have to pay. It is important to find out up-front exactly what you will have to pay so that you aren't overcharged or surprised by hidden fees.

- **What books will I need?** If you need to purchase textbooks, it is important to figure out what the average cost will be ahead of time. You may have to spend hundreds of dollars per course on books, which is something you should find out beforehand in order to add it to your budget. And with a little more research, you might be able to find discounted textbooks online.

- **What hardware will I need in order to participate in the class?** Most online classes require students to have access to a computer that can run the latest word processing programs. If you have an old computer that is not compatible with new programs, you may not be able to participate in an <u>online learning</u> program.

- **Is there any additional software that needs to be purchased?** Many <u>online learning</u> programs provide software for students that can be downloaded free directly from their site, but some programs ask students to buy additional software on their own. This is part of finding out exactly how much you should expect to pay for your class.

- **What's the education and experience of the online instructors?** Your instructors are an important part of your online experience, so make sure to find out as much as you can about them. Most junior college and community college teachers have at least a master's degree in the subject they teach, and the majority of university professors have PhDs. You should look for the same level of education in your online instructors.

- **How many students are in each class?** Classes that are too large make it hard for instructors to work with students who need help. In smaller classes, you have a better chance of getting attention from your teachers. Generally, a class size of about ten to twenty students works best for an online course.

- **How much time does it take to complete the online program?** Some online schools offer students the chance to complete a degree in less time than a traditional degree program as long as they get all the material completed. Because many online programs allow you to work at your own pace, this means that you can move as quickly as you wish.

- **Can I structure the course to my own timeframe?** Although many online programs let students complete assignments at their own pace, others require that students participate in <u>virtual</u> class sessions and have specific deadlines for assignments. Be sure to find out how classes are run so that you can determine if you can truly fit the course work and studying into your schedule.

- **Is any residency required?** Some online programs require students to attend a few classes on a college campus or at another location in addition to completing their online course work. The residency may be one or two weekends or one to two weeks depending on the program and degree. Find out this information beforehand so that you can decide if you'll be able to keep those commitments.

- **Is there extra help if I need it?** Some teachers hold virtual "office hours" online when they are available to students who have additional questions about assignments or need help with them. In other programs, teachers are not available outside of class time.

- **How long has the school/online division been around?** A school that has been established longer is not necessarily a better school, but it is helpful if a school has had some experience with online learning. This includes online divisions of traditional colleges and universities.

- **How many students are currently enrolled and how many students have graduated from the school?** If you enroll in a new online school that has very few students, the program may not be fully developed, and, therefore, might not meet your expectations. In addition, a higher graduation rate shows that more students have successfully completed the program.

- **Is there a Help Desk if I run into trouble with my computer?** Probably the most frustrating part of any online course can be software problems, so it's important to know what kind of tech support is available. This is especially true when you start a program and need to download and log on to the school's interactive management system.

It shouldn't be hard to find answers for these questions either online or by calling the school. Some online learning programs have directors who can answer questions about the program, the teachers, or anything else you wish to know about the school and courses.

WHAT IS ACCREDITATION?

Answering all these questions is important, but if you're planning on earning a degree, the most important homework you can do is to find out if your prospective online school is <u>accredited</u>. Accreditation is the process by which colleges and universities undergo a screening to make sure that their courses meet certain standards of education.

Although the federal government doesn't accredit schools at any level, the U.S. Department of Education and the nongovernmental Council for Higher Education Accreditation (CHEA) monitor colleges and universities that have been <u>accredited</u> by various accrediting associations. The Department of Education and CHEA also monitor regional and national associations that grant accreditation.

Visit http://ope.ed.gov/accreditation/ to find listings of postsecondary institutions that are <u>accredited</u> by agencies recognized by the U.S. Department of Education. The site also lists regional and national accreditation organizations and associations.

Also check CHEA's Web site (www.chea.org/directories/index. asp) to find its list of more than 7,000 institutions and 18,000 programs that CHEA, the Department of Education, or both recognize as fully <u>accredited</u>.

TYPES OF ACCREDITATIONS

Some online schools are regionally <u>accredited</u> and others are nationally <u>accredited</u>. This means that regional organizations focus on schools in a specific area of the country, whereas national organizations accredit schools anywhere in the United States and generally specialize in specific fields.

Regional accreditation is the most commonly accepted form of accreditation for online schools. Most traditional universities and colleges are <u>accredited</u> by one of the six regional organizations in the United States. In fact, until about twenty-five years ago, regional accreditors were the only agencies that <u>accredited</u> degree-granting schools. National accreditors were known for accrediting specialized trade or vocational schools. However, today many national accreditors have expanded their reach and offer accreditation for degree-granting schools. One of the most popular national accrediting organizations, the Distance Education and Training Council (DETC), is recognized as a legitimate accrediting organization by both CHEA and the U.S. Department of Education.

Even so, many regionally <u>accredited</u> schools don't consider nationally <u>accredited</u> schools their equals. So although nationally <u>accredited</u> institutions will usually accept credits from regionally <u>accredited</u> institutions, the reverse is not always true. This could mean that if you have an associate's degree from a nationally <u>accredited</u> school, you may not be able to transfer these credits if you decide to pursue a bachelor's degree at a regionally <u>accredited</u> school.

Why Accreditation Is Important

If you receive an online degree from a school that is not <u>accredited</u>, you may have wasted your money. You might not qualify for a professional license, or you might not be able to meet transfer requirements for higher-level programs. You might even end up losing your job because you lack the required educational qualifications.

Students who pursue degrees in particular fields of study, such as law, medicine, nursing, engineering, and dentistry, need to attend schools that have specialized accreditation. This means that one step in gaining a license to practice in one of these fields is graduation from a school that is <u>accredited</u> by the field's professional organization, such as the American Bar Association or the American Dental Association. (Typically, a prospective candidate must also pass a licensing exam.)

In addition, students can only receive federal financial aid if the institution they are attending has been accredited from an organization recognized by the U.S. Department of Education.

Taking the time to find out if your online school is legitimately accredited will save a great deal of trouble in the long run.

▶ REGIONAL ACCREDITATION ASSOCIATIONS

To determine whether or not an online school is regionally accredited, first find out in which state the online program is operating, and then look to see which regional association grants accreditation to schools in that state. The Web site for each organization lists the schools accredited by that association. For-profit online companies, as well as online divisions of traditional colleges and universities, will be listed.

The following six regional accreditation associations are recognized as legitimate accreditors of online schools as well as traditional colleges and universities. Note that these associations also accredit American and international schools in other countries.

New England Association of Schools and Colleges (NEASC)

Accredits schools in Connecticut, Maine, Massachusetts, New Hampshire, Rhode Island, Vermont, Europe, Africa, Asia, and the Middle East (www.neasc.org)

Middle States Association of Colleges and Schools (MSA)

Accredits schools in Delaware, District of Columbia, Maryland, New Jersey, New York, Pennsylvania, Puerto Rico, U.S. Virgin Islands, Central America, Europe, and the Middle East (www.middlestates.org)

Southern Association of Colleges and Schools (SACS)

Accredits schools in Alabama, Florida, Georgia, Kentucky, Louisiana, Mississippi, North Carolina, South Carolina, Tennessee, Texas, Virginia, and Latin America (www.sacs.org)

North Central Association Commission on Accreditation and School Improvement (NCA)

Accredits schools in Arizona, Arkansas, Colorado, Illinois, Indiana, Iowa, Kansas, Michigan, Minnesota, Missouri, Navajo Nation, Nebraska, New Mexico, North Dakota, Ohio, Oklahoma, South Dakota, West Virginia, Wisconsin, and Wyoming (www.ncacasi.org)

Western Association of Schools and Colleges (WASC)

Accredits schools in California, Hawaii, Guam, American Samoa, Palau, Micronesia, Northern Marianas, Marshall Islands, and other Australasian locations (www.acswasc.org)

Northwest Commission on Colleges and Universities (NWCCU)

Accredits schools in Alaska, Idaho, Montana, Nevada, Oregon, Utah, and Washington (www.nwccu.org)

If you earn a degree from an online school that is accredited by one of these associations, it will be considered as valid as a degree from any traditional college or university.

BE ON THE ALERT FOR "DIPLOMA MILLS"

If you've done some research into online learning, you may have come across the term "diploma mills." What does this mean and why should you stay away from them?

A diploma mill is a fraudulent business that disguises itself as a legitimate online school. It makes money by either offering fake online degree programs or by selling worthless diplomas. Diploma mills end up targeting two kinds of people. The first are students searching for a legitimate academic online program who are unaware that they are enrolling at a diploma mill. The second are people who are aware that the online program is fake, but are looking to build their credentials as quickly as possible for employment or other purposes, and are willing to pay for diplomas and even falsified transcripts.

Diploma mills also do a disservice to employers who unknowingly hire employees without proper credentials. They also can ruin the reputations and enrollments of legitimate online institutions that cannot compete with the instant offers of degrees made by diploma mills.

How Diploma Mills Operate

Anyone who has a good quality color printer and fax, a phone number, e-mail address, and a well-designed Web site can set up a diploma mill. Some diploma mills and unaccredited schools have been able to obtain ".edu" as part of their Web site address, which is easy to do. This makes them look like real schools but actually tells nothing about their quality or legitimacy.

Some diploma mills may steal the computer source code and the design of a real online university, alter the name, and end up fooling many unsuspecting students, even though the Web sites fail to mention an accrediting agency or list a fake accrediting organization. Often, diploma mills use names similar to well-known colleges or universities, such as the University of New York instead of New York University. Many <u>diploma mills</u> change their addresses or move from state to state in order to keep operating.

Because of the relative ease of setting up a <u>virtual</u> school online and because there are now so many legitimate <u>online learning</u> institutions, it has become much easier for <u>diploma mills</u> to function. <u>Diploma mills</u> make millions of dollars a year and new ones are created every day, which makes it hard for educators or the law to keep up with them.

It can also be hard to prosecute a <u>diploma mill</u> if the business acknowledges that it is indeed a <u>diploma mill</u>. The <u>diploma mill</u> can argue that it is only acting as a business and that people who buy degrees are aware that they are getting a degree without having to complete an academic program.

How to Identify a Diploma Mill

It is important to know what you are getting into before you begin any <u>online learning</u> program. Here are some signs that you might be dealing with a <u>diploma mill</u>:

- **You are promised a degree in exchange for a lump sum of money.** If a school states that a degree will cost a lump sum such as $2,000 for a bachelor's degree and $3,000 for a graduate degree, it's not a legitimate online education provider. Legitimate schools, online or not, do not charge flat fees but generally charge tuition by the semester or credit hour.

- **The school's Web site either lists no faculty or faculty who have attended schools <u>accredited</u> by fake accrediting agencies.** Real schools will generally highlight their faculty and staff and post their credentials, which can be easily researched.

- **The online school offers a degree (diploma or certificate) based on life experience when all they require is an evaluation of your résumé.** No valid online learning school will award a degree based solely on a review of career experience.

- **The online school offers a degree in return for cash and a simple requirement such as a ten-page "thesis" or a multiple-choice test.** Earning a legitimate degree requires taking courses as well as preparing assignments and taking tests.

- **Written materials from the online school include numerous spelling and grammatical errors, even on the diploma itself.** Any legitimate school would have staff who could write grammatically-correct and misspelling-free copy for its Web site, brochures, and diplomas.

- **The school stresses how quickly you are able to receive a degree.** Many fake schools offer diplomas in mere days or weeks, based on assessments of previous life experience.

- **The school can only be reached by a P.O. box or by e-mail.** Most legitimate schools disclose their complete contact information, including phone numbers and mailing addresses, on their Web sites and on any registration information. Schools should have an actual physical address, not just a post office box.

- **There is no selectivity in admissions.** As an applying student, you are never asked about your previous academic record. You are never asked to supply transcripts or standardized test scores, and there is no information about transferring already-earned credits to this school.

- **Degree requirements are unspecified.** There is no mention of how many credit hours are required to complete a degree program, and no course descriptions are offered.

Fake Accreditation for Fake Schools

Many diploma mills claim to be "accredited," but they are only accredited by fake organizations (or "accreditation mills") that have been created for just such a purpose. Some diploma mills don't claim accreditation, but do falsely claim how widely their degrees are accepted by other educational institutions, licensing agencies, and various employers. Sometimes, to take advantage of less rigorous laws, diploma mills will sell degrees only in certain states or in other countries. Many diploma mills operate from England, selling fake degrees only to people in other countries, including the United States, Africa, and Asia.

Nonaccredited Online Schools

Not all nonaccredited schools are diploma mills. However, these, too, should be treated with caution. The laws under which online institutions are approved vary from state to state. Some states have high standards, but some states have lax standards or no real ability to enforce their standards. Idaho, Hawaii, Montana, Alabama, Wyoming, Mississippi, and California are known for having lax standards regarding accreditation. This is something to keep in mind as you research online schools.

In addition, only a few states have laws or regulations regarding diploma mills, and accrediting agencies are not in the business of searching out and discrediting diploma mills.

Getting a degree or certificate from a diploma mill is worse than getting one from a nonaccredited school. Students with fake degrees may ultimately find themselves embarrassed professionally if they are found out and may eventually lose their jobs.

How to Safeguard Against Diploma Mills

"Earning" a degree from a diploma mill will not enhance your job prospects if your current employer or a future employer checks and finds out that you have a degree from a diploma mill. It will appear that you are either foolish for not finding out more about the place that gave you your degree or dishonest in trying to pass off a worthless degree as legitimate. What can you do to make sure you are not dealing with a diploma mill? Here are four things that will help you protect your money and your reputation.

- **Find out if the online school you are looking into is accredited and by whom.**

- **Check to see if the accrediting agency is recognized by either the U.S. Department of Education or CHEA.**

- **Check with licensing boards and professional associations to see if the program you are considering is accredited.**

- **Call or write the Better Business Bureau and the attorney general's office to (1) make sure the school is operating legally in a particular state and (2) check if anyone has filed a complaint against the school.**

▶ **COULD THIS ONLINE SCHOOL BE A "DIPLOMA MILL"? CHECKLIST**

For every online school you consider, ask yourself the following questions:

1. Can degrees be purchased online? _____ Yes _____ No

2. Does the school claim to be <u>accredited</u> even if there is no evidence for this? _____ Yes _____ No

3. Is a very short period of time required to earn a degree? _____ Yes _____ No

4. Is there little attendance required of students? _____ Yes _____ No

5. Are degrees available based solely on life or work experience? _____ Yes _____ No

6. Are few assignments required for students to earn credits? _____ Yes _____ No

7. Does the school charge much higher fees as compared to fees charged by higher education institutions? _____ Yes _____ No

8. Or is the fee much lower than that of fees charged by higher education institutions? _____ Yes _____ No

9. Does the school fail to provide information about a campus or location address? _____ Yes _____ No

10. Does the school fail to provide a list of its faculty and their qualifications? _____ Yes _____ No

11. Does the school have a name similar to another well-known college or university? _____ Yes _____ No

If the answers to most of the questions above are "yes," you could be dealing with a diploma mill. Time to do some more homework!

▶ Part II

ONCE YOU'VE DECIDED

Search

Applying to an Online Degree Program

. . . .

"Working online was the least expensive option available to me as well as the fastest course of action. Not only was the course itself accelerated in speed, but the application process was as well. Once I contacted the school and faxed my paperwork to begin as a nonmatriculated student, I was able to begin my studies within a matter of weeks! I began with the start of the next 8-week cycle rather than [waiting for] the next semester or several semesters later."

Marni Tesser
MS, Elementary Education, Hunter College, 1995
Nonmatriculated Student of Special Education,
Grand Canyon University, 2009

. . . .

Let's say you've completed your research and chosen the online degree program that seems right for you. Now it's time to apply to see if you will be accepted. It probably won't surprise you to learn that much of the application process for an online school takes place, well, online. If you haven't applied to a college or university for a number of years, this may be a little different from what you remember. Today, even many traditional on-campus schools offer the option to apply online. Some even require online submission of applications.

STARTING THE APPLICATION PROCESS

Typically, the way to apply for admission to an online school is through the school's Web site. You should look for a link to "Admissions" and click your way there. Not every online school is alike, but generally the admissions section will tell you what materials and information you will need in order to apply. It will also explain whether everything must be done online or if you will need to mail certain items, such as copies of transcripts. The admissions page may also have a link to the financial aid page.

Usually to apply to a school online, you will have to create an account in which you are asked for basic information and are then given instructions on filling out the application. Once you have an account at the online school, you can log in to it as often as you like. When filling out your online application, you will not be allowed to proceed if any information is omitted. This ensures that all required questions are answered on the application.

Some schools allow you to check your application status online about ten days after submitting it.

THE TESTS YOU MAY NEED TO TAKE

Even before filling out the application for an online degree program, it is important that you find out what information you will need to supply. It is important to find this out as soon as possible so that you are able to meet the application deadline. Required information may include grades from previous degree programs, if applicable, and test scores such as the SAT, ACT, or GRE, depending on the degree program to which you are applying.

Most traditional colleges and universities require standardized tests as part of their admissions process, but some accredited online schools do not. Some are more interested in your work experience or grade-point average from previous degree programs. It is worth doing a little research beforehand to find out if the online schools you are applying to require standardized tests scores. If they don't, you can save yourself time and money. If they do, here are some of the tests you should know about.

Undergraduate Tests

Bachelor's degree programs, both traditional and online, usually require a standardized admission test, either the SAT or the ACT. These tests are used as a standard by colleges and universities to predict how well students might do at the school and to compare all the students who are applying to their school.

The ACT

The ACT consists of four content-based tests: English, math, reading, and science reasoning. The scores range from 1 (lowest) to 36 (highest). The ACT used to be more commonly accepted by colleges and universities in the Midwest, but now many schools nationwide accept either ACT or SAT scores.

Contact www.actstudent.org to find out information about ACT registration, dates, and fees.

The SAT

The SAT tests math and verbal reasoning skills and problem solving. The SAT consists of three parts: critical reading, mathematics, and writing. The scores from each section can range from 200 (lowest) to 800 (highest), and the highest composite score is 2400.

Contact www.collegeboard.com to find out information about SAT registration, dates, and fees.

The SAT Subject Tests

The SAT Subject Tests are one-hour multiple-choice tests in five subject categories: English, mathematics, history and social studies, science, and languages. In all, there are twenty tests such as World History, Chemistry, Chinese with Listening, and German. Many colleges and universities use the Subject Tests for admissions and for course placement once students have been accepted.

Contact http://professionals.collegeboard.com/testing/sat-subject to find out information about SAT Subject Test registration, dates, and fees.

Graduate Tests

There are also exams for entrance into graduate programs.

The GRE®

The GRE®, which stands for Graduate Record Examination® General Test, is usually needed to apply to most graduate degree programs. It consists of three sections: verbal, quantitative, and analytical writing. The verbal and quantitative sections are set up similarly to those sections on the SAT, but they are more challenging. The analytical writing section consists of two essay questions.

Your prospective graduate program may place more importance on certain sections of the GRE® depending upon the subject area you plan to study. For example, if you are applying for a master's degree in English, your verbal and analytical writing scores may be weighted more than your quantitative score.

Contact www.ets.org/gre to find out information about GRE® registration, dates, and fees.

The GRE® Subject Tests

Some graduate programs request that their applicants take the GRE® General Test, or a GRE® Subject Test, or both. The GRE® Subject Tests are offered in the following subjects: biochemistry, cell and molecular biology; biology; chemistry; computer science; literature in English; mathematics; physics; and psychology.

Visit www.ets.org/gre/subject/about for information about GRE Subject Test registration, dates, and fees.

Professional School Tests

Entrance into a master of business administration program, as well as entrance into law school and medical school, requires passing specific exams.

The GMAT®

The GMAT®, or Graduate Management Admissions Test®, is a standardized test business schools use to assess their applicants. The GMAT®, like the GRE®, consists of three sections: verbal, quantitative, and analytical writing assessment, though the content of each section is somewhat different than that of the GRE®.

Contact www.mba.com/mba/thegmat to find out information about GMAT® registration, dates, and fees.

The LSAT

The Law School Admission Test, popularly known as LSAT, is a standardized test that applicants to law school must take. The LSAT has five 35-minute sections of multiple-choice questions, plus a writing section. The writing section is not scored, but a copy of it is sent along with a person's application to law schools.

Contact www.lsac.org/LSAT/TheLSAT-menu.asp to find out information about LSAT registration, dates, and fees.

The MCAT

All medical schools require the Medical College Admission Test, or MCAT, as part of the admission process. The MCAT is known for being one of the most challenging standardized tests given. It has three multiple-choice sections—verbal reasoning, physical sciences, and biological sciences—plus a writing section, which consists of two essay questions.

Contact www.aamc.org/students/mcat to find out information about MCAT registration, dates, and fees.

COMPLETING THE APPLICATION

Once you know which tests you need to take and when, you will be ready to fill out the application for your online school. If you are applying for a bachelor's degree program, there are two options for applications—the college's or university's own application or the Common Application. The school's Web site will tell you which one you have to use. Sometimes a school will require the Common Application and also some pages from its own application.

The Common Application is a standardized college application form that is accepted by approximately 400 colleges and universities nationwide. Once you fill out the Common Application, you can send it to any school that participates in the program. You won't need to fill out a different form for each school.

Check your prospective school's Web site to see if they use the Common Application or visit the Common Application Web site at www.commonapp.org/CommonApp/Members.aspx and look through the list to see if the school is a member. If so, fill out the Common Application.

Practice Run

If you have never filled out an online application before, you can print out a sample and complete it by hand before transferring the answers to the online application. If your application requires an essay, write out a draft of your essay in a separate document, then copy and paste the essay into the online application. Make sure that when you are filling out the application, you have enough time to go through it slowly and carefully.

Application Fee

Most colleges and universities charge an application fee, which typically ranges from $35 to $60. This fee is usually nonrefundable—

even if you aren't admitted to the school. Not surprisingly, many schools allow you to pay this fee online.

Transcripts

Whether you are applying to the online division of a community college, four-year college, or graduate school or to an online school, you will need to send copies of official <u>transcripts</u> from any schools you have previously attended. This typically includes high school and any postsecondary institutions. Contact your previous schools directly and their guidance office or registrar will tell you what you need to do in order to have your <u>transcripts</u> sent.

Letters of Recommendation

Not all online schools request letters of recommendation, but some schools, especially graduate schools, require two or three recommendations from a teacher, counselor, or someone else who is familiar with your academic work. However, a number of online degree programs designed for adult learners will allow you to use letters from employers. These schools recognize that many applicants have been out of school for a while. If the information is not available in the online admissions section, call or e-mail the program to which you are applying in order find out if this substitution is acceptable.

No matter who will be writing your recommendations, you should always ask for letters early so there is enough time to get them in before the application deadline. Give each person a deadline that is two or three weeks before the letters are due. You should also send out e-mail reminders as the deadline approaches. Today, many schools provide a secure Web site for letter writers to use to complete and e-mail their recommendations.

The Essay

Some online degree programs require their applicants to submit an essay with their applications. This allows schools to get a better sense of their applicants and also helps to determine each student's writing ability. The essay topics vary greatly. Some schools require a personal statement from each student (this might be called a Statement of Purpose). Other schools have specific questions they want their students to answer in an original way.

Though not all online degree programs require an essay, you should not choose a program simply on the basis of whether or not an essay is required. Your online degree program, no matter what discipline it is in, will require writing. So even if you don't have to write an essay to apply, you will definitely be required to write once you are accepted.

TIPS FOR WRITING A PERSONAL ESSAY

The five-paragraph essay is a good model to use. It includes a one-paragraph introduction, three paragraphs in the body of the essay, and a one-paragraph conclusion. If you haven't written an essay in a while, the following tips will help you organize your ideas into a winning essay—one that will win you a spot in your program of choice:

- Read the essay question or prompt carefully. Restate the question in your own words to make sure you understand exactly what you are expected to write about.

- Choose a method to organize your essay. Most questions can be answered by chronological order, order of importance, or compare and contrast. Do you want to explain events based on chronological, or time, order? Would it be better to arrange your ideas from most important to least important? Or, would showing differences and similarities among your ideas be a better approach to writing your essay?

- List the details you want to include in your essay.

- Create an outline of these ideas based on your method of organization.

- As you write your draft, remember to include an introduction to state the purpose of your essay, enough supporting details in the body of the essay to make your points clear, and a conclusion.

- Reread the question to make sure you answered the question. Revise as necessary.

- Ask others to read your essay and give you feedback. If any points are unclear, make sure you clarify them in your final draft.

- Proofread your final version for spelling, grammar, and punctuation. Once you are satisfied with your essay, copy and paste it into your online application.

TRANSFERRING CREDITS

If you are considering an online degree and you've already earned some college credits, you should consider transferring those credits to your online school. This can save you both time and money. However, because online degree program requirements vary, check before you enroll to make sure transfer credits are accepted. If not, you will have to take those classes over or find a different online school that will accept them.

In general, only credits from an <u>accredited</u> college will be accepted. This is especially true if you are transferring credits from another online school. <u>Accredited</u> online program credits are no different from credits earned at traditional colleges. If the online school is <u>accredited</u> by an authorized accrediting agency, your course credits should be transferable.

There are other conditions that might restrict your ability to transfer credits. If you took a class that is not part of your new degree program, the credits might not be counted. It also depends upon how many credits your courses were worth. If your previous school offered three-credit courses and your new school has four-credit courses, your prior credits might not be transferable. In addition, some schools may not accept courses with grades below a certain level. You should keep all of this in mind as you begin to research transferring credits to your new school.

LIFE EXPERIENCE

Many undergraduate online degree programs will give credit for knowledge and skills applicants have gained through life or work experience. Usually, to earn this kind of credit, you will need to assemble a portfolio of information about your work, which could include writing samples, official job descriptions, written or taped presentations, military records, and awards. Your online degree program's Web site should provide information about awarding credits for life experience.

It is also possible to earn credit for life experience if you take certain exams to assess your knowledge in specific areas. The CLEP, or College-Level Examination Program, is probably the best known standardized test program of this type. The CLEP tests usually consist of multiple-choice questions, though some have essay sections. The tests generally cover what students take in their first two years of college. Visit www.collegeboard.com/student/testing/clep/about.html to find out more about this exam.

Students can also earn college credit by passing DSST exams, or DANTES Subject Standardized Tests. The program began as a service of the Department of Defense for service members and their families. However, anyone may now take the tests and earn college credit.

WORK AND MILITARY TRAINING

If you have ever taken courses through your employer or served in the military and received specialized training, you might be able to receive college credit that you could apply toward a degree program. The American Council on Education (ACE) College Credit Recommendation Service evaluates work training programs and, based on certain criteria, will recommend college credit if the programs meet the standards. If you have taken courses through your employer, visit www.acenet.edu/resources/memberdirectory to find out if you can earn college credit for them.

▶ **APPLICATION TIMETABLE CHECKLIST**

To streamline your application process, fill in the date when each task is due. Then as you accomplish the task, check it off. Create a timetable for each application you're sending.

Task	Due Date	Completed
☐ Reviewed online degree programs		
☐ Chose program(s) to apply to		
☐ Application forms downloaded/ printed		
☐ Standardized tests scheduled		
☐ Standardized tests taken		
☐ Test scores requested		
☐ Transcripts requested		
☐ Letters of recommendation requested		

☐ Letters of recommendation reminders e-mailed   _____ _____

☐ Letters of recommendation submitted   _____ _____

Task	Due Date	Completed
☐ Essay(s) written	_____	_____
☐ Application submitted online	_____	_____
☐ Application fee(s) paid	_____	_____
☐ Application status checked	_____	_____
☐ Notification of acceptance	_____	_____
☐ Registered	_____	_____

Paying for Online Learning

"When I first started my associate degree online, I was working part-time so my yearly salary was low. On top of that, I had three kids at home and my daughter was also starting community college. I was eligible for a federal Pell Grant, which covered the expenses for the courses and some toward my books. Not long after, I was changed to full-time at work . . . so I didn't qualify for the grant anymore. Rensselaer County has a policy that they will pay for up to 6 credits a semester for an employee to attend the local community college if it is pertinent to your job. As I was going for a degree in Liberal Arts, I was covered for each semester. The only thing I had to pay for myself was books."

Sue Jones
AA, Individual Studies, 2006
Hudson Valley Community College

"My employer agreed to reimburse me for 25 percent of the tuition costs for my online certification course, although some students taking the course were covered 100 percent in advance by their employers. But this certification was really my idea, and I was going to do it, with or without reimbursement."

Jason Malfatto
Graduate Certificate in Human Computer Interaction,
2008 Rensselaer Polytechnic Institute

Once you've decided you're ready to try <u>online learning</u> and have figured out what online school or program you need, the next question you should ask yourself is: How am I going to pay for it all?

LOOKING AT THE COSTS

The truth is, <u>online learning</u> can be expensive. First, there is tuition to consider. Then there are textbooks, supplies, and additional software if your class requires it. If your computer is not up-to-date, this might be yet another cost you'll need to add. You will also need to figure in the cost for a high-speed Internet connection, if you don't already have one.

Just as the cost of earning a traditional degree varies greatly between public and private schools, online course costs also vary. One credit hour at a community college could cost $80, 1 credit hour at a public university could cost $200, and 1 credit hour at a private university could cost $1,200. Certificate programs that take a year or two to complete range from $2,000 to $4,000 for tuition. The cost also depends on where you are studying—university, community college, or technical institute.

Luckily, options exist that can help you reduce the costs for your online education, including <u>financial aid</u>, loans, <u>grants</u>, <u>scholarships</u>, and even Web sites that can help you get good deals on textbooks and free downloads of software. Before paying for everything out of your own pocket, do some homework and see what options you might have.

FUNDING OPTIONS

If you have already chosen the <u>online learning</u> program(s) that you want to apply to and you'd like to talk to someone about <u>financial aid</u>, you can't go wrong by calling or e-mailing the <u>financial aid</u>

department. Here you will find someone to guide you through the best financial aid programs and payment options for your particular needs.

However, if you are just starting out and don't yet have a particular online school in mind, the best first step is to visit Student Aid on the Web at http://studentaid.ed.gov/. This site, hosted by the Department of Education, provides detailed information on various financial aid options for college and graduate students.

FAFSA

You should also fill out a Free Application for Federal Student Aid (FAFSA) at www.fafsa.ed.gov. Federal Student Aid, an office of the Department of Education, is the largest source of student aid in the United States. The application on the office's Web site, which can be completed online or printed out and mailed in, is used to determine the amount that a student can be awarded for all federal, state, and school-sponsored aid programs.

Not all online schools are eligible for federal student loans. In order for students to receive financial aid from the federal government, online learning programs must be accredited and must meet other criteria established by Congress. To find out if a prospective online school participates in federal student loan programs, you should contact the school directly.

Suppose the school you are applying to does participate in these programs. To qualify for federal student aid, you need to

- demonstrate financial need.

- be enrolled as a regular student in an eligible program.

- be a United States citizen (or eligible noncitizen).

- have a high school diploma or a GED.

- be enrolled or accepted as a student working toward a degree or certificate in an eligible program at a school that participates in the federal student aid programs, which includes online schools.

- have a valid Social Security number.

- be registered for Selective Service if you are a male between 18 and 25.

- not have a drug conviction for an offense that occurred while you were receiving financial aid.

In general, financial aid is usually limited to students who take online courses and programs for credit, but some noncredit certification programs are also eligible for financial aid. The best thing to do is fill out a FAFSA application and see what your options are.

Grants

A grant is an award that is given to students to fund their education and does not have to be repaid. Grants may be awarded by public or private institutions and corporations.

Pell Grants

The most common education grant is the Pell Grant, which is awarded by the U.S. government. Pell Grants are based on financial need, but there are other requirements as well. To be eligible, students

- must be undergraduates.

- must be working on their first undergraduate degree.

- must attend a federally approved school.

- cannot be incarcerated.

Award amounts for Pell Grants depend on a number of factors, including tuition cost, family income, part-time or full-time student status, and whether a student will be attending school for the full academic year. The maximum Pell Grant per student is determined by federal law and increases slightly on an annual basis. For the 2010–11 school year, the maximum was $5,550 per eligible student. As a result of a law passed in 2010, the maximum Pell Grant going forward will increase on average at an annualized rate of 0.75 percent less than the Consumer Price Index. By completing a FAFSA application you can find out if you are eligible for a Pell Grant.

State Grants

State grants for education are another option. A number of states provide grants to students, and if you live in one of these states, you may qualify. Some state grants are based on financial need, but some may be based on other factors, such as grants for older students returning to school for continuing education, or for specific academic programs.

For these grants, you need to apply directly to your state's commission on higher education. For more information on each state's financial aid programs, grants, and scholarships, visit the Education Resource Organizations Directory, which provides links for each state and for U.S. territories, visit http://wdcrobcolp01.ed.gov/Programs/EROD/org_list.cfm?category_ID=SHE.

Tuition Reimbursement

Another option is to find out if your employer will help finance your online learning. Many employers will pay for college courses or certificate programs that are directly related to their business. Some employers give preference to employees who enroll in online degree programs because they know that this option can be done on the employee's own schedule and will not likely affect the employee's time at work.

Employers usually have specific requirements regarding tuition reimbursement for employees. If you are interested in exploring this option, you should check your company's policies and procedures manual, or check with the human resource-office to find out details.

Federal Loans

If you are not eligible for a federal grant, you may want to consider applying for one of two federal education loan programs. The Stafford Loan is a fixed interest rate loan for undergraduate and graduate students who attend an accredited school at least half-time. There are two kinds of Stafford Loans, subsidized and unsubsidized. The former is need-based, and the latter is not. No money has to be repaid as long as a student is in school. Students may combine Stafford Loans with scholarships, grants, and work-study awards.

Through 2011, Stafford Loans will be offered by the Federal Family Education Loan program. However, after this time, Stafford Loans will become part of the Direct Loan program. The only thing that will change for students is that the loans will come directly from the federal government through college financial aid offices instead of from private lenders who previously acted as intermediaries for some student loans. The eligibility requirements and the need to complete the FAFSA remain the same.

Another federal loan option is the Perkins Loan, which is a low-interest student loan for undergraduate and graduate students in great financial need. Like the Stafford Loan program, no repayment is required while a student is enrolled in school, and other financial aid may be combined with a Perkins Loan.

To apply for both the <u>Stafford Loan</u> and Perkins Loan programs, you must fill out a <u>FAFSA</u> application (www.fafsa.ed. gov). For specific details on each program, consult the U.S. Department of Education Web site at http://www.ed.gov/.

Private Loans

If you find you still need money to pay for an online degree, you may want to consider a private loan. These are loans provided by banks, nonprofit organizations, and other financial institutions. Your school's <u>financial aid</u> office can provide you with details about various private loans.

A student's eligibility for a private loan generally depends on his or her credit score as opposed to financial need. (Credit scores are not considered for federal loans.) Interest rates for private loans are usually higher than those for federal loans, but the application process takes little time, and payment will be made directly to you, not to the school. Although private loans can be used to cover all or nearly all of your educational costs, it is important to remember that these loans will have to be paid back with compounded interest. It is wise to consider a private loan only after you have explored all other options.

Loan Forgiveness

If you agree to pursue a particular career or work for a certain amount of time in an underserved area, you may be able to get help paying for your education. Some professions, including law enforcement, nursing, and the military reserves, are in serious need of new members. Other professions find it difficult to attract people to certain geographic areas. For example, there may be a surplus of teachers available to teach in suburban school districts but a lack of teachers in urban districts. In fact, in certain circumstances, the federal government will cancel all or part of your federal student loans. This is known as loan forgiveness. Here are some options to consider:

- The Teacher Loan Forgiveness Program was set up to encourage students to pursue careers in teaching. Under this program, people who teach full-time for five consecutive academic years in schools that serve low-income families can become eligible for loan forgiveness. http://studentaid.ed.gov/PORTALSWebApp/students/english/cancelstaff.jsp?tab=repaying.

- On the American Federation of Teachers Web site, you can search for loan forgiveness programs, teacher grants, and awards. www.aft.org/yourwork/tools4teachers/fundingdatabase/index.cfm

- The Department of Defense's Troops-to-Teachers program provides money to recruit and support former members of the armed forces while they obtain certification to become teachers in high-need areas. www.ed.gov/programs/troops/index.html

- The G.I. Bill of Rights Web site, www.gibill.va.gov, lists all educational benefits for veterans provided by the Department of Veteran Affairs.

- Law schools may forgive the loans of students who pursue law careers in public interest and other nonprofit areas. The American Bar Association offers information about loan repayment assistance programs and loan forgiveness. www.abanet.org/legalservices/sclaid/lrap/home.html

- The National Health Service Corps offers loan forgiveness to doctors who agree to practice for a certain number of years in high-need areas that lack adequate medical care. www.nhsc.hrsa.gov

- By participating in the Nursing Education Loan Repayment Program, nursing students can get a portion of their education loans repaid. www.hrsa.gov/loanscholarships/repayment/nursing

- Some volunteer organizations such as AmeriCorps and the Peace Corps also offer <u>loan forgiveness</u>. Visit the following sites to find out more: www.americorps.gov/for_individuals/benefits/index.asp www.peacecorps.gov/index.cfm?shell=learn.whyvol.finben

Tax Benefits

You should also be aware of tax benefits related to education. For example, the Hope Scholarship Tax Credit allows taxpayers to claim eligible dependents for up to two years for the purpose of claiming this credit. Students who are enrolled at least half-time and have not completed their first two years of undergraduate study qualify. Households that have no tax liability because their incomes are too low may file a tax return for a refund of up to $1,000.

The Lifetime Learning Tax Credit kicks in for juniors, seniors, graduate students, and working adults returning to school to improve their skills. Families can receive a 20 percent tax credit for the first $10,000 of tuition and fees for all eligible students. This means that the maximum amount of a Lifetime Learning Tax Credit is $2,000. This tax credit is available for all years of postsecondary education, as well as for courses or certification programs related to improving job skills.

You may also qualify for a student loan interest deduction on your taxes. This entitles qualified student borrowers to deduct the interest they pay on a loan taken out solely to pay for higher education expenses.

More information on eligibility and the benefits of tax credits related to education can be found at the IRS Web site: www.irs.gov/publications/p970.

▶ GREEN LEARNING: SAVING MONEY AND THE ENVIRONMENT

Did you know that getting an online degree actually benefits the environment? In fact, you might call online learning "green learning." Just think about the nature of online learning: online students travel less, if at all, and do not use on-campus resources, including student housing, the cafeteria, and the classrooms. In addition, there is little paper used in online learning, which reduces the number of trees cut down as well as the energy consumed in the production and transportation of paper and paper goods.

In a study conducted by the Design Innovation Group at Open University in England, the researchers found that, on average, online learning courses "consumed nearly 90 percent less energy and produced 85 percent fewer CO2 emissions. . .than the conventional campus-based university courses." The researchers found that even pursuing a degree partly online cuts energy consumption and CO2 emissions.

According to a study by San Jose State University in California, if the 46 percent of its students who drive alone to campus replaced one day of commuting with completing their assignments online, the result would be 6,351,003.48 fewer pounds of carbon dioxide produced each semester and $1,043,194.12 less spent on gas per semester. What a huge difference a single day of online learning can make!

In 2008, the Montana university system took going green seriously and established the Montana Green Campus (mtgreen.

mus.edu). Montana's colleges and universities collaborate to offer more than fifty online degrees each semester and over 500 online courses. Students matriculate in one college or university but may take courses online from any member of the university system. Many of the online programs offered are in "green" industries, such as green technology, environmental restoration, and renewable energy.

OPTIONS FOR TEXTBOOKS

"Most of my professors have assigned e-books for their courses, although some still prefer the $300 hard covers."

Dennis Wizeman
MBA, 2012
University of Montana

College textbooks are expensive. While some online schools offer reading material free of charge, most still require students to buy traditional textbooks. Depending on the courses you're taking and the number of different textbooks required per course, the cost of textbooks can end up totaling even more than the tuition for your online courses. But you don't have to spend as much money as you may think.

One of the first steps you should take in saving money on textbooks is to register early for your courses. That way you can get your booklists early and will have plenty of time to look for bargains. For each book, make sure you have the title and edition; the author's name; the book's ISBN, which is the letters "ISBN" followed by a series of numbers found on or near the barcode on the back of the book; and the price of the book. This information will help you begin your online research. If your booklist includes only some of this information, you can search for the rest of it online.

Free Textbooks

Once you have the information, see if you can find any of the materials you need online for free. There are a number of online libraries that offer free reference articles and books, though usually this is for older materials with expired copyrights. Most of these sites allow you to download the books for free and then view them on a desktop computer or a handheld device.

The Internet Public Library (www.ipl.org) offers links to hundreds of books, magazines, and newspapers. Another site, Bartleby (www.bartleby.com), has thousands of e-books and reference materials available. Project Gutenberg (www.gutenberg.org/wiki/Main_Page) allows you to download over 30,000 e-books free, including famous classic novels and texts. Google Scholar (scholar.google.com) also offers a large collection of e-books and free academic articles.

Another option for free books is, of course, the library. It is unlikely that your local public library carries textbooks, but you can try an interlibrary loan, which will allow you to request a book from any library within your library system. If your reading list includes fiction or nonfiction works, the library is a good option. You may be able to take out books for the whole semester or at least for as long as you'll need them, but check the library's policy before you take out the books. If you end up having to pay a late charge for overdue books, you could wipe out part of your textbook savings.

If the library does not have the current edition of a text but has a previous edition available, you may be able to use it. It is likely that the previous edition has much of the same information as the new edition. To be safe, check with your instructor to see if using a previous edition is an option.

Cheap Textbooks

If you can't find your books free online or at the library, you should still be able to find them for less than their retail price.

First, you might want to check PDX Books, www.pdxbooks. com. This site lets you to type in the title of any college textbook and then gives you an instant list of various online bookstores and their prices. You can also search the Web sites of online bookstores and compare prices that way, but make sure you add shipping costs when making a final comparison. It is also important to find out the return policy of any online bookstore, in case you need to return the book for some reason.

Also, used books are almost always cheaper than new books, so you might want to consider looking online for a used book that's in good condition. You can also hunt around local used bookstores for your textbooks, especially used bookstores near campus.

You might also try to find students who bought the books for your courses during a previous semester. If your online school has message boards, you can search for students who have taken the course before and are willing to sell the book to you at a cheaper price.

Renting Textbooks

There are also some online sites that allow you to rent textbooks for a certain period of time, such as a semester, a quarter, or a summer, which is much cheaper than buying them. If you rent a book for a semester, your rental period begins on the first day of your class and ends 130 days later, when you must return the book. There is also an option for buying books that you rented, if you choose to keep them.

E-Book Editions

Some college textbooks are now available online as e-books. You can either access these for free or for a much lower cost than traditional textbooks. If you are considering purchasing an electronic version of a textbook, you should know that unlike actual hardcover textbooks, e-books cannot be returned. In addition, access to e-books may expire after a period of time, and some publishers limit or restrict your ability to print from an e-book.

Reselling Your Books

Once your course has ended, you might think about reselling your books if you don't plan to use them again. You can try to resell them to the same place you bought them, whether it was a campus or local bookstore or an online bookstore. Or you could place a notice on a message board asking if any students about to take the course are interested in buying them.

Online Textbook Sources

Here are some Web sites you might consider when searching online for the best prices for textbooks and academic articles:

> www.alibris.com/books/textbooks
> www.amazon.com
> www.bartleby.com
> http://www.ebay.com/ or www.half.ebay.com
> http://www.gutenberg.org/
> www.ipl.org
> scholar.google.com
> www.textbookx.com

FREE SOFTWARE

Most online courses will provide a list of required software. Typically, you will need basic word processing and spreadsheet software in order to begin. These programs should have come with your computer at the time of purchase. However, you may need to upgrade the programs from the free installed versions to later editions or to Microsoft Word and Excel if you have some other word processing and spreadsheet programs. These will not be free.

Beyond the Basic Software

There may be a few more programs that you will need to download before you begin your online classes. Antivirus software is very important to ensure that your computer and documents are safe. There are plenty of online sites that allow you to download antivirus and antispyware software for free.

You may also find that a PDF reader, such as Adobe Acrobat, is necessary to view many reading materials online. The latest version of Adobe is usually available as a free download online.

You might also need to download a media player, such as RealPlayer, Adobe Flash Player, Apple Quicktime Player, or Windows Media Player, that will allow you to view video and audio materials. These are also available as free downloads online.

Finally, you may also need to download an unzipping software program. The ZIP file format is a way to compress files so that you can store or send large files in a reduced file size. There are various free unzipping software programs available to download on the Web that will allow you to both zip and unzip files as necessary. Some service providers have this function built into their e-mail systems. Check yours to find out.

These software programs may be all you need. However, be sure to check with your syllabi to find out if there are additional software programs you will need to download for free or purchase in order to participate in your class. If you do find more software required for your course, it wouldn't hurt to do some research online to compare the best prices, just as you will do for textbooks. (The school's online management system such as <u>Blackboard</u> or <u>Moodle</u> will be a free download.)

▶ PAYING FOR ONLINE LEARNING CHECKLIST

It is important to plan ahead to determine how much your <u>online learning</u> is really going to cost. Use this checklist to help you determine the total cost.

Tuition: _____

Additional fees: _____

Textbooks: _____

Additional school supplies: _____

Home office/study space set up: _____

Monthly Internet connection: _____

Updated computer hardware, if needed: _____

Additional computer software: _____

Miscellaneous expenses: _____

*Subtotal: _____

TOTAL: _____

*If you are receiving any <u>grants</u>, <u>scholarships</u>, or other sources of funding related to your online education, subtract the amount to find your total out-of-pocket cost.

▶Part III

WHAT TO EXPECT

Search

Your Online Learning Experience

· ·

"One of the surprises I have had about online learning is how hard it is and at the same time how rewarding. I am no stranger to hard work, but this is the most challenging thing I have ever done. I first started out thinking I could handle a full course load with a baby at home. I soon learned that two classes were enough to do at a time."

Laura Wall
BS, Applied Mathematics, 2010
Empire State College

· ·

· ·

"A few years ago I was looking at the possibility of changing careers to become a children's librarian. I decided to take a few courses in library science. I chose online courses because of the convenience of being able to do the work on my schedule, a huge help to a mother of an infant, and also because doing the work online allowed me to take courses from a community college in another part of the state. The opportunity to explore a new career while completing assignments and tests at home on my schedule worked very well for me."

Mary Susan Milbourne
Online Courses in Library Science, 2005
Northampton Community College

· ·

. . . .

"Some professors know how to teach effectively online, and others do not. I have spent a good deal of time listening to some professors talking with the tech guy about problems with Blackboard or Moodle, or looking at just half of an Excel spreadsheet because the professor did not know he needed to resize when sharing his desktop. On the other hand, there have been some professors who have been extremely well prepared, and seamlessly integrated their PowerPoint [presentations] and spreadsheets into the class in a much more effective way than a 'live' professor might be able to."

Dennis Wizeman
MBA, 2012
University of Montana

. . . .

You may be wondering what your online experience will really be like. How much work will you have to do? How will you communicate with your professors and fellow classmates if you aren't in a classroom together? How will you work on group projects with your classmates? In order to answer these questions, it's best to go over some of the basic parts of your online learning experience. To begin with, where's the best place for you to log on and to study?

IF NOT IN A CLASSROOM, WHERE?

Because you won't be taking your classes in a classroom, where should you be while you are logging on for video lectures, live chats, discussion boards, etc.? The local coffee shop with WiFi? The couch with the game playing in the background? The kitchen trying to get lunch for a hungry, crying toddler? No to all of these if you want to be successful.

Home Study Space

Having an entire room set aside just for you would be ideal, but that isn't always possible if you live with roommates or have a family. One possibility is to set up a home office area or study space in a part of the house that isn't used very often, such as the attic or basement. You want an area that is not heavily trafficked, so that people won't be constantly walking through and distracting you. The kitchen is usually a poor choice for logging in to your classes or studying because there is potential for noise and traffic there. If you live in an apartment and the only possibility is your bedroom, try to fit in a desk even if it's a plank over two file cabinets—some place to put your computer and keep the books and papers you'll need for your classes.

To set up your home office or study space, create a list of all the items you will need. Here are some of the basics:

- desk and chair.
- desktop or laptop computer with a high-speed Internet connection.
- printer and/or scanner.
- floor lamp or desk lamp.
- filing cabinet.
- supplies, such as notebooks, pens, paper, highlighters, and sticky notes and storage space for them.

Make sure your work area is always fairly neat so you can start working right away when you sit down without having to search for what you need or being distracted by clutter. Everything should have a place on your desk or in file drawers so you will always be able to find things easily and not waste time hunting them down.

Public Space

The problem with distractions is that small noises will only become magnified when you are trying to concentrate on writing a paper, posting to a discussion board, or studying for an exam. If noise becomes a problem, you may want to purchase headphones or ear plugs.

If they don't work, or if you can't make a dedicated study space at home, consider places outside your home, such as a library or a college study center. However, if you are participating in a live synchronous online class, make sure that you will have both uninterrupted time and a lack of distractions so you can participate.

SOME ONLINE COURSE BASICS

First, even before you begin an online class, make sure you understand how your technology works, including your word processing software, e-mail, Internet browser, and any other technology you might need for your class. Should you experience any problems with the technical aspects of your online course (such as your password or login information or e-mail), get it resolved as soon as you can. Even waiting a few days will make it harder to meet any deadlines that you have.

An online class will require a minimum of six to ten hours a week—and some people report spending fifteen to twenty hours a week. Even if you don't study every day, you should log in every day to read e-mails from your instructor and fellow classmates or to participate in online discussions.

Your instructor will also be checking in online regularly in order to post information about the class and to respond to questions or comments from students. It is important to stay in touch with your instructor and make sure to let him or her know as soon as possible if you are having trouble with the class or assignments.

Many online course providers offer support services to help students, such as tutors to help with course work and tech support staff to help with technical or administrative issues. If you need help, do not hesitate to take advantage of these services.

A word to the wise: make sure to back up your work. Save your work regularly as you are writing, and then save all your files not just on your hard drive but also on a CD or DVD or memory stick. This way if anything happens to your computer's hard drive, you will not lose all your work.

▶ STUDY TIPS FOR SUCCESS

There is no "best way" to study. It is something that comes with trial and error; what works well for one person may not work for you. But here are some suggestions to try that could make your online learning experience more successful.

Setting Up a Schedule

- **Create a study plan for yourself.** Instead of studying many hours one day, none the next day, and then a few hours the day after that based on your other activities, come up with a schedule so that you know exactly how many hours a week and when you will be studying or doing online work. If it's not possible to study every day, at least try to spend the same amount of time on the days that you will be studying.

- **If your only study time at home coincides with when your family or roommates are also home, make sure everyone knows your study schedule and when you cannot be**

interrupted or disturbed. Put your study schedule up on the refrigerator or other communal <u>message board</u> so your household will know your study routine.

- **Create a calendar of your assignments and make sure to review it each week.** Perhaps every Sunday night, go over the deadlines for your classes for the coming week. Are any upcoming papers due or are there online exams? This way you can make sure that the work gets done that week.

Getting Down to Work

- **Get rid of as many distractions as possible.** The top distraction for many people is the phone. To maximize your participation in online classes and minimize your distractions, turn off the ring tone and vibrate function on your cell phone.

- **When you begin a study session, do the work that requires the most concentration first, such as reading assignments.** This tactic will ensure that you have enough energy to tackle the hardest work. If you are taking more than one course, make sure to spend time on your most challenging course every day and work on it before your other courses.

- **Try to study in 20–40-minute blocks of time followed by a break.** Exactly how long you should study is different for each student. Try to figure out what works best for you. Some students get restless after a short time and need more breaks and other students can go for longer times without breaks. If the reading material is difficult, you may require more frequent breaks.

- **During your study breaks, make sure you really relax.** Take your breaks away from your desk or wherever you are studying. Use the time to think about other things and not about what you have just studied.

- **Postpone anything that can be put off until your school work is finished for the day.** This might be a challenge, but other activities will actually be more enjoyable without the pressure of an assignment hanging over your head.

HANDS-ON LEARNING. . .ONLINE!

There might not be a huge difference in taking a history or business course in person or online, but what about science courses in which labs make up an important part? How do online classes deal with the hands-on part of learning?

Many online classes include online video demos or <u>tutorials</u> to help students visualize necessary information. However, if you're taking an online chemistry class or a continuing education workshop for paramedics on improving blood drawing skills, you may need to go one step further.

One option is the <u>hybrid course</u>. Some courses use a combination of online instruction and on-campus time. For an online chemistry class, students might watch an instructor's lectures via streaming video, complete all their homework assignments and quizzes online, and then go to campus two or three times a semester to complete their lab work. A workshop on blood drawing skills might involve an online <u>tutorial</u> and then a day at a lab.

Some science courses use simulation software for labs. Students interact with animated equipment in a way that is similar to a real lab experience. They virtually choose the lab materials, proceed through the lab, and then watch simulated reactions. Students then send their results to their instructor via e-mail, and the instructor evaluates each part of the lab and grades the student.

Some online chemistry courses allow students to conduct lab experiments in their own homes. University of North Carolina,

Wilmington, chemistry professor James H. Reeves and University of Colorado, Denver, chemistry professor Doris R. Kimbrough created a series of experiments for introductory college chemistry courses that can be done at home. These experiments rely on common household ingredients, such as baking soda and vinegar. According to Reeves, students who performed these simple chemistry experiments at home did just as well on their chemistry exams as those who took part in traditional chemistry labs on campus.

TAKING ONLINE QUIZZES AND TESTS

Online courses for degrees and certification typically include online quizzes and tests. There are different types of online tests, but they are usually very easy to navigate and require only that students have high-speed Internet connections.

In degree courses, some instructors may give weekly online quizzes that are multiple choice or true/false. Some may require essay tests only at the end of the semester. Every instructor provides a course outline at the beginning of the class that will include the dates of any online quizzes and tests. One of the advantages of online exams is that you usually receive your results instantly.

You can take online tests with all your books and reading materials nearby for reference, but that doesn't necessarily make them easier. You might have to answer 50 questions in 30 minutes, for example, and then the test will time out. That means answering one question every 36 seconds, so there won't be enough time to look up many answers. Just as with a traditional course, if you aren't prepared, you won't be able to do well on the tests.

Continuing Education and Certification

. . . .

"For my real estate license, I was required to complete a specific number of continuing education credit hours. The programs that offer real estate courses send mailings to agents a few months prior to when their license is up for renewal. I was given the option of completing the requirements online, which was more time efficient, so that is what I chose. . . . Once the course work was fulfilled it was a very simple and easy process for getting verification of course completion. It was sent electronically to the state licensing agency, which made getting my new license very speedy."

Julie Sasso
Licensed Real Estate Agent
New York State

. . . .

Online certificates and continuing education courses often include quizzes throughout the course work and conclude with a final exam that must be passed in order to receive certification or continuing education credits. Often this score will be sent directly to the governing body that issues the certification.

Usually you are able to review all the course material at your own pace. Then at the end, there will be a link to a test to take. In some cases, you will have to go through sections of a presentation, taking and passing a quiz in order to proceed to the next section. Once the test is completed, you will receive your score.

▶ TIPS FOR TAKING ONLINE TESTS AND QUIZZES

The following are some tips to help you with online test-taking. The first and most basic tip is: READ THE INSTRUCTIONS CAREFULLY because they tell you important information.

- **The instructions will tell you if the test is timed and if you can save your results and return if you are interrupted.** Usually if you quit in the middle of an online test, it will be stored and graded as is. Sometimes, however, you can return to the test at a later time. Before you begin your test, read the instructions to find out what will happen if for some reason you have to quit the test before you are finished.

- **If you are required to go straight through the test with no breaks, do not begin until you are certain you won't be interrupted.**

- **Check to see if you need to answer all the questions in sequence or if you can skip some and go back and answer them at the end.** You may be able to use "next" and "previous" buttons to move back and forth through the test questions.

- **See if you can change answers, and if there is a "review" feature that lets you check your work at the end of the test.**

- **Make sure you know how to save your answers on the test so that they aren't lost.** You might have to click a button at the end that says "complete the test" after all your answers have been filled in.

- **For online tests that include short answer and essay questions, you might want to write your answers in a**

word processing file, and then copy and paste them into the test question. The test instructions should tell you if this is possible.

- Finally, make sure you know how to receive your score and how your score will be sent to your instructor and any other place you may need to have it sent.

LIVE CHAT SESSIONS

. . . .

"Availability is an important part of online learning. Having chat room hours provides a forum for students to approach a professor in a less formal atmosphere. Plus it's in real-time for both parties. For a struggling student who needs help, it can be a last resort that can bring progress. Online chatting is a growing part of online learning that can include video conference, file sharing, polls, and other features. Professors and students should embrace these technologies, and those who are new to these resources should test them out to make sure they're comfortable beforehand so they don't miss out on the rewards of such experiences."

Ameerah Cetawayo
Adjunct Instructor, Governmental Accounting
Schenectady County Community College

. . . .

Virtual discussions are a big part of taking a class online. Because there is usually little or no face-to-face contact with your instructor and fellow students, online communication has to take its place. Online classes often have discussion boards, in which students can post comments, ask questions, and talk to one another and to the instructor about a variety of topics relating to their online course. These live chat sessions can take place in a variety of ways.

- Text chat. This is the simplest kind of chat session in which participants log on to their computers at the same time and join in a discussion by typing in comments.

- Instant messaging (IM). Students and instructors use personal computers or mobile phones to instant message each other. They can exchange messages privately, as they would using e-mail, or join group discussions. IM allows users to send photos, video files, and other attachments.

- Voice chat. Voice chat allows the instructor and students to meet "live" online from their computers, using a microphone for two-way voice communication, in addition to text chat.

- Video and audio chat. This is also known as videoconferencing or Web conferencing, and it provides the most realistic form of communication in real time. Participants communicate using voice, text, and video through Web cams or streaming video.

Virtual discussion rooms may be very familiar if you're used to IM, or they could be something completely new. If you are taking an online class, you should expect to attend some live chat sessions with your fellow classmates and instructors.

Chat Session Do's and Don'ts

Be On Time
Probably the most important thing is to be on time for your chat session. Your instructor will specify in advance when it will take place, so be sure to schedule it on your calendar. If you know

you're going to be late, however, let your instructor know, or see if there might be another time the session can be scheduled. If you simply show up late, it's the same as showing up late to a live class. Everyone will notice and you will make a bad impression. If you are given a choice of chat times, be sure to pick a time when you know you will not be interrupted.

Be Prepared

Come prepared to your chat session. The form it takes may seem a little different, but chat sessions function like classroom discussions. In an actual classroom, you need to be prepared to discuss the topic at hand and it's the same for an online chat room. Most instructors will post the topic for the chat room beforehand in the assignments, so be sure and read the assignments required for that session.

Ground Rules

In the beginning of each chat session, most instructors will go over the rules, such as time limits and what is and is not acceptable. Make sure these rules are clear to you. The chat room is where your instructor gets to see you interact with others, and you want to make a good impression. Your participation in chat discussions is likely to be part of your overall grade, just as classroom participation is part of your grade in traditional classes.

Netiquette

There is a certain etiquette, or "netiquette," to participating in online chat rooms. You need to make sure you are polite and respectful to everyone online. This means waiting until others are finished "speaking," that is, inputting their thoughts. Some people are very slow typists, or they might not have a high-speed Internet connection. Your instructor will moderate and make sure things move along smoothly. You can always review the material if the chat is going really slowly.

Also, you should never use inappropriate or intemperate language. This is something that your instructor will be sure to make clear before the chat begins.

During Your Chat Session

Make sure you have your books and any other background material readily available when you participate in your chat session. This way you can refer to the material to support your points, and to help you get a better idea of the points being made by other students in the <u>chat room</u>. If you want to refer to something specific in a reading in your comments, just refer to the page in the book or article. You don't need to type in the text of the reference.

It is important to keep focused while you are participating in a virtual chat session. Avoid the temptation to check your e-mail or to surf online while the discussion is taking place. You may miss important information, or you may not be able to answer immediately if someone writes something to you directly.

Make sure that when you post a comment during a chat, you read it over before submitting it. Spelling and grammatical errors will not make a good impression. In addition, make sure you never dash off something quickly in anger if you disagree with someone. Always try to write when you are calm and have thought through your ideas and their implications.

Be prepared for the unexpected. Sometimes technology can be unpredictable. Something might happen to cause you to lose power or the class Web site could go down. Also, something might come up at the last minute causing you to miss your chat session. If something happens, be sure to e-mail your instructor as soon as you can. If you had to miss the chat session, make sure to ask how you can make it up.

A Side Benefit of Chat Sessions

If you find it easier to study with a partner or in a group, you might want to think about getting together with other students in the class. During your chat session, if you feel that a person or people in the group might be helpful to you, don't be afraid to set up additional study times with them. Some people in your group might understand things that you don't.

You can also compare notes with other group members. This will help you fill in information you missed. Talking about information with other people will help you remember the points better. Even if you live far away from your classmates and can't get together in person, you can e-mail or IM one another about your readings or class discussions.

WEBINARS

. . . .

"For my job, I participate in Webinars at least once every other week to keep up-to-date on all the latest government program changes and technical training. Usually you are sent an e-mail with the Web link and then you proceed to the site at the scheduled time. A presenter narrates a slide presentation for about an hour. During the presentation there is a chat window in which you can type in questions or [orally] ask questions and receive your answers in real time."

Tina Carton
Capital/Saratoga Energy Smart Regional Coordinator

. . . .

A Webinar, or Web-based seminar, is a type of Web conference in which people participate in meetings or presentations over the Internet. Webinars are often used for continuing education credits, and may be offered regularly to keep people updated on the latest developments in their fields. Sometimes an online course may consist of a series of Webinars, with exams at the end.

In order to participate in a Webinar, your computer must be able to run the necessary Web conferencing software, which is often available free online for downloading. Participants will receive an e-mail about the Webinar that includes the link that will connect them to it, plus the technology requirements.

During the presentation, participants may be allowed to contribute oral comments or questions or write them in a chat window in real time. Sometimes, however, the question-and-answer portion is saved until after the presentation is over.

As with any type of chat session, it is important to be prepared beforehand and to make sure you are focused and attentive. It is also important to set the time aside so you won't be interrupted during the Webinar.

WORKING IN VIRTUAL GROUPS AND OTHER FORMS OF TEAM WORK

. . . .

"During some of our lectures, the instructor would divide the class into separate work groups to collaborate on solving a problem. We would have 20 minutes or so before we had to present our solution. . . . Once we figured out how to share our desktops and/or programs with the Web conferencing software, Adobe Connect, we were able to use other, more suitable, software (PowerPoint or Visio) to present the results to the entire class."

Jason Malfatto
Graduate Certificate in Human Computer Interaction, 2008
Rensselaer Polytechnic Institute

. . . .

"We functioned surprisingly well as a group because the digital setup at the school was quite sophisticated. There were many mailboxes in which different activities took place, so the students had a place to dialogue with one another. There was a place where I could draw over their drawings to correct them and a place for me to write comments about the work. When they had to do a paper, they could go online to look up an artist's work and then report back. We emphasized a personal response . . . and, depending on the level of the student, we got a variety of responses, some quite good."

Mona Mark
Instructor, Online Education Department
Academy of Art University

Not only are virtual chat sessions part of the <u>online learning</u> experience, but some online classes, especially in business schools, include a group component in the course work. Students are required to work together to either solve a problem or create a project or presentation. This enables students to learn from one another, helps them develop a sense of community, and allows students to get used to leading a team of peers.

You might have no problem sharing ideas and discussing the course readings in chat sessions or on <u>discussion boards</u>, but working on an online group project may seem a bit more intimidating or complicated. What if no one does the work but you? What if everyone tries to be the leader of the group? How can you really talk about the project when you never meet face to face? What is the best way to master a virtual group project?

The Nature of Group Projects

The goal of a group project is generally to produce a written paper, presentation, or a media project. Usually your instructor will assign students to groups of three or four and you will be expected to produce a project together. Often the project requires the creation of a PowerPoint presentation or another type of media presentation involving online tools. Your group might have to work together in a short time period, or you might have a group project to present at the end of the semester.

Group interaction should be based upon mutual respect and encouragement, just as it would be during any kind of class discussion. A group project should always be a cooperative, not competitive, learning experience. The group should manage to incorporate the ideas of all individuals.

However, problems arise. Some members in the group could become angry if they feel the workload is not evenly distributed, or if they feel that some people are not following the agreed-upon schedule. On the other hand, some team members may attempt to dominate and not allow everyone to contribute equally to the project. It is important to make clear at the beginning exactly what each person is responsible for and how to contact one another if problems or questions arise.

Organizing the Work

The first thing to do after you find out the requirements for your project is to get in contact with your group members. It's probably best to communicate in real time if you can, either with instant messaging, live chat, or video chat. Discuss what is required and what the final project will look like. To make it easier, break the project into steps and, if possible, have each member of the group handle one of the steps.

One of the biggest problems facing group projects is working out schedules and time commitments. Everyone is likely to be working on a different schedule, and it can be hard to coordinate the timing of joint work sessions. It's important that everyone in the group agree to all the deadlines. You might want to schedule weekly check-ins, if the project is semester-long.

Sometimes you may be asked to write a group paper, in which everyone contributes, but the final paper is to be read as a complete work. This can be challenging to accomplish because everyone writes differently, and the paper may not read very smoothly if the voice continually changes. One way to deal with this situation is to break the paper into parts, so that each part can be written by a different person and different writing styles will not matter as much. The paper can be presented as group collaboration with clearly defined parts.

Benefits of Group Work

Working in an online group does present some challenges that may not occur in traditional classrooms, but these challenges are not insurmountable. You are already self-motivated enough to tackle the specific challenges of online learning. You can use this strength in your work with your fellow students, all of whom are likely dealing with similar challenges.

It is most important in group projects to make yourself heard, to contribute as much as you are required, and to bring up any questions or problems as soon as you see them. The skills that you develop by working in your virtual group can be carried with you into your career and your life.

▶ CREATING YOUR LEARNING ENVIRONMENT CHECKLIST

Before you begin any online course, you should make sure that you have set up your study space, created your study schedule, and informed your family and friends what you're doing. The following checklist will help you get ready. Check off all that apply to your situation. Aim to have everything checked off before you begin your first class.

☐ My study space is in a quiet location where I'll have few distractions from phones ringing, music playing, or people talking or walking through.

☐ I have eliminated distractions such as a TV or gaming system.

☐ I can close the door to my study space and have time to myself.

☐ The desk in this space is comfortable enough and set up for studying.

☐ The chair is comfortable but not so comfortable that I can fall asleep easily.

☐ The lighting is just right for reading both books and on screen.

☐ I have a place to keep all of my study materials so I can start work immediately when I sit down.

☐ The space is comfortable enough and I can see myself studying here on a regular basis.

☐ I have made a note for myself on my desk to remind me to turn off my cell phone when I sit down to work.

☐ I have set up a schedule for completing my online course work and studying.

☐ I have given members of my household and friends my schedule and asked them not to interrupt me while I'm studying.

Chapter 8 `Go`

The Tech Side of Online Learning

. . . .

"My college used Blackboard [management system] for online classes. Blackboard made things really easy because you would just log on every day, find the homework, check the discussion board, and submit your work, all on the same site."

Karen Goldfarb
BS, Psychobiology, 2007
Binghamton University

. . . .

. . . .

"Each course in my online program was split between distance students and on-campus students, so the on-campus students and instructor would have to speak into a microphone so we distance students could hear them. The lecture room had to be wired for distance and required at least one audio-visual technician to operate several cameras and to troubleshoot any technical problems with the broadcast. Each distance student was given the Web site address and a personal log-in account. Joining a lecture was as simple as going to the Web site, logging in, and navigating to the lecture page at the specified time."

Jason Malfatto
Graduate Certificate in Human Computer Interaction,
2008 Rensselaer Polytechnic Institute

. . . .

Part of the online learning experience is, of course, the online part. But you don't need to be a computer geek to take an online course. However, you should probably be familiar with using a computer and navigating around the Internet before getting started.

It is also important to make sure that you have the right computer equipment and software. Generally, if your computer is fewer than five years old, it should be fine. But there are some computer requirements and skills that you should have before you register for an online course. Luckily it won't take long to figure out if you have the hardware and skills that you'll need.

COMPUTER REQUIREMENTS

"I did not need to purchase any technology before I started my class, except a required downloaded version of the textbook. . . . My academic adviser took me on a guided tutorial of the system the online school used for accessing information, submitting course work, course communication, and performing library research."

Marni Tesser
MS, Elementary Education, 1995
Hunter College
Nonmatriculated Student of Special Education, 2009
Grand Canyon University

"I purchased a wireless router, which was not really required, but since it allows me to access the Internet in any room in my house, it made working around my family's movements easier."

Dennis Wizeman
MBA, 2012
University of Montana

So what kind of technology do you really need for <u>online learning</u>? As you will see, most of what you'll need are things that came with your computer. Depending on the course, you may need to purchase or download some extra software, but you probably already have the basic technology.

Hardware

The following is a list of hardware items that can affect your ability to participate in an online class:

- **System Unit.** The <u>system unit</u> is the core of the computer, which for a desktop is usually a rectangular box, or tower, that goes on or under your desk. The <u>system unit</u> may also be so small that it's contained inside a laptop. The <u>system unit</u> contains the processor and the memory, the things that make the computer run.

- **Processor.** The processor, which is the heart of the <u>system unit</u>, dictates how fast your computer can run its programs. Most online courses require that you have a processor that operates at 300 MHz or higher.

- **Memory.** In order to store information, such as software programs and files, a computer needs a large amount of available, or unused, memory. The amount of memory affects the speed of a computer. The more memory a computer has the faster it can run its programs. Most courses recommend that your computer have at least 128 MB of <u>RAM</u> (random access memory).

- **Monitor.** Some online courses may require you to view documents that have been scanned in. Your monitor should be large enough to allow you to see all images on the screen clearly and legibly. This could be a problem if you are trying to view a spreadsheet on a Netbook.

- **Disk Drive.** Desktops and large laptops have CD and/or DVD disk drives as part of the internal <u>system unit</u>. These internal disk drives allow you to download course materials and save them on something other than your hard drive. However, some of the smaller computers like Netbooks do not have internal disk drives. In that case, you will need to purchase a <u>memory stick</u> or an <u>external disk drive</u>.

- **Modem.** You will need an <u>Internet service provider</u> (<u>ISP</u>) such as cable or <u>DSL</u> to connect your modem to the Internet. Dial-up connections will be too slow to handle the demands of an online class. A modem with a <u>baud rate</u> of at least 56 K is usually the minimum requirement.

- **Sound Card and Speakers.** Some online classes will require you to view audio and/or video files. In order to hear the sound on these, you will need a sound card and speakers installed on your computer. You may also want to get some headphones, so the sound does not disturb anyone around you. Some of the smaller computers don't have speakers, so you'll need headphones no matter where you are taking the course.

- **Printer.** You may want to print out some of your course information or research materials. For this, you will need a printer that can print graphics clearly, such as an inkjet or laser printer. A color printer isn't necessary, but some people prefer them anyway.

Software

Software requirements can vary greatly from course to course. Some online courses in art, math, computer programming, and business may require special software in order to complete your assignments and projects, but your instructor will tell you before the course begins what you need. Some of the software may be free downloads.

The basic software that you will need for any online course includes the following:

- **Operating System.** The operating system controls the execution of the computer's programs. You will need an up-to-date operating system, and your instructor will likely specify which operating system you will need. Generally, if you are using a PC, you will need Windows XP or higher. If you are using a Mac, you will need OS.X 10.1 or higher.

- **Word Processor.** Word processors are the programs that give you the tools that allow you to write, edit, and format documents. The most commonly used word processing program for both PCs and Macs is Microsoft Word, and generally most online courses require you to use it.

- **E-mail Account.** You will need an e-mail account in order to send and receive e-mails. Your school may provide you with one, but if it doesn't, think about setting one up that is different from the one you use for personal or work e-mails.

- **Web Browser.** A Web browser is a software program that allows you to access Web sites. The most popular are Internet Explorer, Mozilla Firefox, and Apple Safari. Your computer is likely to have come with a browser installed, but any of these, as well as others, can be downloaded free from the Internet.

- **Plug-Ins.** Plug-ins are software programs that allow you to open different types of files, such as audio, video, or other <u>multimedia</u>. If you need any plug-ins for your course, your instructor will provide you with a list. Plug-ins, such as Adobe Acrobat Reader, Windows Media Player, QuickTime Player, and RealPlayer, are usually available as free software downloads from the Internet.

▶ ONLINE COURSE MANAGEMENT SYSTEMS

Many colleges use online course management systems, such as <u>Blackboard</u>, <u>ANGEL</u>, and <u>Moodle</u>, which allow students to access course materials, visit <u>chat rooms</u>, and find assignments and grades, all on the same Web site. All a student needs is a computer and a high-speed Internet connection.

If your online school uses a course management system, your instructors will give you information about which of the features you will be using in their courses. In order to participate in any <u>online learning</u> system, you will need to know how to open and save files, send and receive e-mails with attachments, upload files, and navigate around the Internet. Many online schools provide an orientation or <u>tutorial</u> for using their specific course management system.

In order to use a management system like <u>Blackboard</u>, students are given a link to the school's own <u>Blackboard</u> Web site. Students are also provided with personal log-in information in order to enter the site but will not be able to log in to their courses until the first day of classes.

When you log in to the Web site, you will have access to your own personal home page, which will enable you to access all the courses in which you're enrolled. Each course has a course menu that will link you to course documents, assignments, <u>discussion boards</u>, grades, and other information.

In addition, some online course management systems use Course Mail, which is a way for instructors and students to communicate without using personal e-mail accounts. By using Course Mail, you can receive all e-mails related to your courses in one place. You don't have to worry about school messages getting lost in your spam folder. You can log in to the Web site to view your course mail or, if you prefer, the course mail can be forwarded to a personal e-mail account.

ANTIVIRUS PROGRAMS

In addition to software that can help you open video files or browse the Web, you will also need certain software programs to help protect your computer. These programs help keep viruses and spyware from infiltrating your computer, slowing it down or worse, deleting data.

Computer Viruses

A computer virus is a human-created computer program or code that attaches itself to a file or another software program. Computer viruses become active when a person opens an infected file sent by e-mail or downloads an infected program from the Internet.

Some computer viruses are designed to interfere with how your system operates, and others try to copy themselves and then spread to other computers. Any type of computer virus is dangerous because it can corrupt and damage your files.

However, viruses can only infect your computer through a human action, like opening an infected file or executing an infected downloaded program. Because of this, there are certain safety practices you should get in the habit of following. Here are three important ones:

- **Never open e-mail attachments that look suspicious.** Even if you know the sender of the e-mail, you should still use caution (1) if you didn't expect to receive an attachment from this person, (2) if it seems odd that this person would be sending an attachment on this subject, or (3) if the e-mail itself is obviously one that has flown around the Internet among people you've never heard of. You can always contact the sender to make sure the e-mail was really sent from him or her. Some viruses can simply pull e-mail addresses from your computer and use that address as the sender, even if the e-mail really came from another account.

- **Use caution when downloading free software, music, or other programs from the Internet.** Many sites that provide free downloads are safe and secure, but others may end up putting your computer at risk for infection. You can always check online for reviews of any free downloaded material and see if there are warnings about certain sites.

- **Pay attention to prompts about virus updates.** Like viruses that affect humans, computer viruses often adapt to their surrounding conditions. If a way to combat a virus is discovered, the virus may alter itself in order to work around it. System operators, such as Microsoft and Apple, try to stay on top of the latest viruses. Often you will receive automatic prompts for online updates that will be sent to your computer's operating system. These updates include the latest information about computer viruses. Execute these updates when they appear.

Despite these precautions, you may still become an unknowing victim of a computer virus. This is the reason you should also have antivirus software installed on your computer.

Antivirus Software

There are many antivirus software programs available and most of them are relatively inexpensive. Many are even available as free downloads from the Internet.

Antivirus software is regularly subjected to independent reviews that evaluate how effective the programs are in keeping viruses from infecting computers. If you're trying to decide which antivirus software to use, you should do some research and read reviews of antivirus programs online or in computer magazines.

The two most commonly used antivirus software programs are products by McAfee and Norton, part of Symantec. Basic versions of their antivirus software are available online free for downloading. These will give your computer limited antivirus protection.

McAfee and Norton also have more sophisticated versions that you have to pay for and that give your computer additional protection. These programs are available for an annual subscription fee and entitle the user to frequent updates to block or search for and remove viruses. The solutions are downloaded automatically to your computer during the life of your subscription.

Sometimes you can use a trial version of antivirus software before purchasing it online. If you do this, make sure to renew your subscription before the trial expires or you could leave your computer unprotected.

How Antivirus Software Works

Antivirus software programs scan for new viruses when you go online and also scan downloaded files from the Internet before you open them. This means that the antivirus program should be running on your computer at all times. Some programs run by themselves, but others need to be executed. You should check your computer to make sure that your antivirus software program is always running.

Antivirus software programs also contain files that define all the new viruses out there in order to search for them. If this file is not updated, your program will not be able to recognize any new viruses that appear. Most antivirus programs search for new virus definitions automatically, as part of their virus scans, but some programs require that you update them yourself. This should be done at least once a week.

ANTISPYWARE PROGRAMS

Spyware is a type of software that that collects bits of information about computer users without their knowledge. Usually, spyware is secretly installed on people's computers as they browse the Internet and visit certain sites. Spyware programs collect various types of personal information, such as Internet sites that people visit, in order to redirect their Web browsers to specific advertising sites.

Spyware can change your computer settings, slowing down your Internet connection speed and even causing other programs to malfunction. Because of this, it is highly recommended that anyone who uses the Internet install antispyware software on their computers.

Antispyware Software

There are many antispyware software programs available for free downloads on the Internet. Just as you would with antivirus software, you should look up reviews of antispyware software before deciding on one to install.

If there is an antispyware program for sale and also a free version of it, this is usually because the company wants you to try the free version first and then upgrade to the for-sale version. This means that the free version of the software will have fewer features than the version that is for sale.

However, some antispyware programs really are free. Some of the most popular ones are Spybot Search and Destroy, Ad-Aware, and Windows Defender. It is actually recommended that you use two different antispyware programs, so that one catches the spyware that the other misses. If you are using free antispyware programs, it is easy enough to download two different programs. The programs should always be regularly updated and run on a regular basis to remove spyware from your computer. Often you cannot set antispyware programs to run automatically, so you will have to remember to run these programs about once a week.

POP-UP BLOCKERS

Like spyware, adware is secretly installed on your computer as you browse the Internet. Adware usually opens pop-up ads and it can also redirect you to advertising sites.

Because of the prevalence of spyware, adware, and other pop-up advertising on the Internet, most Web browsers include tools that block pop-up windows from appearing on your computer. However, most online course management systems, like Blackboard and Moodle, use pop-up windows as part of their e-mail, online quizzes, and discussion tools. If this is the case, you should check your browser settings before you start your class and disable all <u>pop-up blockers</u>. After your class is over, you can turn them back on.

GENERAL COMPUTER SKILLS YOU SHOULD HAVE

In addition to basic hardware and software, there are some basic computer skills that people who take online courses should have. The day your course begins is not the time to figure out how to use a Web browser.

Here are some basic skills you should come prepared to class with. You need to know how to

- copy and paste text into a document.

- create, store, and retrieve Word files.

- set up an e-mail account.

- send and receive attachments.

- navigate your way around the Internet using a Web browser.

- download and install software from the Internet.

- use a CD-ROM, DVD, or <u>memory stick</u>.

COURSE-SPECIFIC COMPUTER SKILLS

There are also some specific skills you might have to learn once you begin your course work. For example, some courses may require you to use spreadsheet, database, and presentation software such as Excel®, Access®, and PowerPoint®. If you are not familiar with how to use these programs, you can perform a quick search online for free <u>tutorials</u> that can walk you through each one.

You might also want to learn about chat, or the real-time discussions you will be having with your instructor and fellow classmates during your online class meetings. Using chat is very easy, but if you are not familiar with online chat, you might want to take the time to learn about it before your first online class. There are free <u>tutorials</u> online that can show you how to use the chat function in an online course.

In general, you should always try to familiarize yourself with an online class before it begins. Do not wait until just before the class starts to log in to the course. If you already have a username and password, you can log on a few hours before the first class meets to look around and get used to the environment.

HELP FROM THE HELP DESK

Finally, during an online class or during your study time, you might experience a computer failure, such as a hard drive crash. Although this is not very likely to occur, it is important to think about what you could use as a backup in such a situation. Can you borrow a friend's computer? Can you use the computer in your local library? Think about your options in case you need somewhere to go in an emergency.

In addition, if your online school has a help desk, you should familiarize yourself with it before any problems arise. That way, in an emergency, you will know whom to contact right away.

▶ COMPUTER TECHNOLOGY CHECKLIST

Before you take an online class, you should be confident about your computer skills and/or aware of what you need to learn. Check off the following computer skills and information that you already have. Then aim to check off everything on the list before your classes begin.

- ☐ I have checked to see that my computer meets the minimum requirements for online course work.

- ☐ I have access to a computer 5–7 days a week.

- ☐ I know how to send and receive e-mails and attachments.

- ☐ I know how to do basic word processing, including cutting and pasting.

- ☐ I know how to connect to the Internet using a Web browser.

- ☐ I can navigate around the Internet and know how to use search engines.

- ☐ I know how to download software from the Internet and/or from CDs and DVDs.

- ☐ I know how to log on to my online course.

- ☐ I know how to back up my files.

- ☐ I am willing to learn about new technology or new computer skills for my online class.

Sourcing Your Work and Avoiding Plagiarism

WHAT IS PLAGIARISM?

· ·

"Plagiarism was an issue but only with a small percentage of students. . . . There were personal mailboxes and when students seemed to have problems of any kind I would have a private dialogue with them and this worked surprisingly well."

Mona Mark
Instructor, Online Education Department
Academy of Art University

· ·

· ·

"I follow my university's plagiarism policy strictly. Students who make the effort to be dishonest will automatically fail. It is to no one's benefit when a student plagiarizes material. It is easy to spot someone who is plagiarizing: details in assignments that don't match the same level of complexity in class discussion or a lack of consistency in the level of performance overall. Those are obvious red signs. Luckily, many colleges and universities use plagiarism software, and there are plenty of free programs available online [to check student work]."

Ameerah Cetawayo
Adjunct Professor, Governmental Accounting
Schenectady County Community College

· ·

What exactly is <u>plagiarism</u>? The Council of Writing Program Administrators (www.wpacouncil.org/node/9) states: "In an instructional setting, <u>plagiarism</u> occurs when a writer deliberately uses someone else's language, ideas, or other original (not <u>common knowledge</u>) material without acknowledging its source." This simply means that if you present someone else's words and ideas as your own, you're guilty of <u>plagiarism</u>.

Students <u>plagiarize</u> for a variety of reasons. <u>Plagiarism</u> can be intentional; a student deliberately uses another's work. Some students leave the writing of their research papers until the last minute and then feel there is no other option except to use someone else's material. Other students lack confidence in their own writing abilities and feel the need to use the work of others.

<u>Plagiarism</u> can also happen unintentionally. As students quickly copy and paste from various sources, they may intend to insert quotation marks and <u>citations</u> later on, but they never do. Or they may simply not know the proper way to cite references.

Not surprisingly, <u>plagiarism</u> is considered a very serious offense at all schools, whether traditional or online. Students can fail a course because of <u>plagiarism</u> or, in the case of repeated <u>plagiarism</u>, they can be suspended or expelled.

Clearly <u>plagiarism</u> is something to be avoided at all costs. The best way to avoid it is to learn exactly what it is and how to properly cite your sources.

THE PROBLEM OF PLAGIARISM WITH ONLINE SOURCES

Just as with any type of source—print book, ebook, magazine, newspaper, scholarly report, research study—if you're going to use online sources, you must document them. There are two reasons for this:

1. You must give credit to the people whose ideas and information you are using. If you don't document your sources, you are basically stealing that information from them and passing it off as your own.

2. Citations provide a way for your readers to look up your sources. By providing your readers with a list of sources, you make it easier for them to consult them for more information on the topic or to use the sources later for their own papers and reports.

There are a number of ways students can plagiarize material:

- **By downloading a free research paper from the Internet.** Usually research papers on the Web were written by other students and have been shared among many. Free research papers are often of poor quality and may even be recognized by instructors because they do not match the class work or the writing style of the student. Also, software is now available that enables instructors to check papers against research reports floating around the Internet.

- **By purchasing a research paper from a Web site that specializes in selling them.** These papers are usually of better quality, though sometimes they are suspiciously too well-researched and written, and instructors can easily recognize that they are not their students' work.

Instructors can also browse these Web sites and search for papers by subject or title.

- **By copying an article from a Web site or an online database.** These papers may be well-written but may not include many citations. The writing style may also be a clue that it was not written by the student.

- **By copying papers from students who have previously taken the course.** If an instructor keeps copies of previous papers that were turned in, he or she can easily tell if an old paper has been copied. Again, there are the issues of writing style and the student's own work which the instructor can compare with the research paper.

- **By cutting and pasting from various sources to create a paper.** These papers are usually obviously plagiarized because the tone changes from passage to passage and the citations are not consistent. Also, if the student includes something original in the paper, his or her style will be noticeably different from that of the rest of the paper.

- **By making up quotations or citations.** Some students will go so far as to invent quotes or source materials. Instructors can easily detect this practice simply by checking citations in the paper.

- **By ignoring copyright notices.** Web sites typically are copyrighted, and this means the information on the Web site is copyrighted. Typically, a copyright notice appears at the bottom of the page that indicates how the information may be used by others. Ignoring this notice and using the information as though it were your own is not only plagiarism but is also a violation of the law, that is, a crime. Material on government Web sites—federal, state, and local—may be used freely by anyone, but a proper citation needs to be included.

- **Sometimes students try to cite their sources properly but incorrectly use quotation marks or don't understand the correct citation form.** Though neither is intentional, they both unfortunately count as plagiarism.

CHOOSING RELIABLE ONLINE SOURCES

. . . .

"Plagiarism is a big problem both online and in the regular classroom. In terms of papers, I try to work with the students on an incremental approach in which they commit to variables, hypotheses, and methods, little by little. Then when it's time to write their paper it's hard for them to find something online that is exactly what they already started. I also stress to my students that we are, ultimately, on an honor system. It is not hard to pass my class if you do the work, so there is no need to cheat."

Moises Salinas
Associate Professor, Psychology
Central Connecticut State University

. . . .

Plagiarizing another's words and citing unreliable sources in a report have both undoubtedly been happening since the first scholar assigned a research report to students. The proliferation of information on the Internet has simply made it easier to cut and paste someone else's work. You don't even have to type it.

At the same time, there is an unlimited amount of both reliable and unreliable information available online. The Internet has also given rise to all sorts of bogus, slanted, and exaggerated information. If students do not know how to find good resources online, they might enter a search term into Google and look only at the first few searches that come up. Some students choose whatever documents they find that make their point and never bother to check the authenticity and accuracy of the information or the credentials of the author. "It must be true; I read it on the Internet" has taken the place of "It must be true; I read it in a book (heard it on the news)."

• •

"I tell my students that the Internet is a marvelous tool for research, though it must be used critically and carefully. A good rule of thumb is to stick to Web sites where the authorship and date of page publication is clear; at a minimum, they should be able to find the page author's name, credentials, current job, and contact information on the page. I also tell them to use some common sense. If it doesn't look, sound, or feel like a credible source, it probably is not. And always, if they have any questions, they can ask me or our friendly reference librarians for help in locating better sources."

Bridgett Williams-Searle
Associate Professor, History
The College of Saint Rose

• •

How can you determine if an online source is reliable? There is no easy answer. For example, even if your source comes from a library database, this does not mean that the articles you will find there are necessarily unbiased or accurate. Just as you would for any print material, it is important that you check each online source carefully.

In general, when searching through online Web sites, here are some things to look out for:

- **The Web site should state clearly which company, institution, or organization is responsible for the information on the site.** There should be a link that describes what the company or organization does (such as an "About Us" or "Mission" link). There should also be real-time contact information available on the site.

- **The Web site should clearly state who wrote the information.** Even though you may find factual information on a Web site, if there is no author listed it is harder to validate what is presented. If an author is listed, what do you know or what can you find out about this person? If you are reading information on a college or university site, check the educational level of the writer. Choose a professor, instructor, or teaching assistant, in that order, over an undergraduate.

- **The Web site should also clearly state when the information was written.** If the information is several years old, it may be out-of-date. What was once true may no longer be true.

- **There should be cited (or linked) sources for all factual information, and the source material should include some non-Internet sources.** The lack of any supporting evidence is the best indication that the material is not reliable—unless it is clearly stated as the writer's opinion.

- **The writing on the Web site should be free of grammar and spelling errors.** Most careful writers check their work for grammatical errors and spelling mistakes. Even if the errors come from carelessness, it still indicates that the Web site may not be credible.

- **You should be able to find other sources that support the information on the Web site.** If you are looking for factual information, it is a good idea to find at least three sources that agree. If the sources do not agree, you will need to do further research on the credibility of the source or on the information presented before you can be certain the facts are accurate. If you are looking for people's opinions, you still need to find facts to support those opinions.

- **The Web site should not be biased or try to persuade the reader to a point of view.** Some information may appear to be presented objectively but may have a hidden bias or agenda. It is important to get a sense of the intention of the organization hosting the site from the tone of the writing, the examples used, or the type and placement of advertising.

What's the URL?

You should also pay attention to the URL ending of Web sites. For example, if a Web site ends in .gov, it is most likely a reliable government site. These sites are good sources for governmental reports and statistics.

If a Web site ends with .edu, it is most likely an educational institution. However, this does not mean that it will be free of bias. Educational institutions may have particular agendas. In addition, it is not all that hard to buy an .edu domain, meaning that a company can simply use an .edu ending to make it seem more legitimate.

Web sites that end in .org are usually nonprofit organizations. They can be good sources of information related to their specific missions. However, nonprofits can also have political agendas and biases, so you need to check the information carefully.

Using .com sites is not necessarily a bad idea. Many .com sites include advertising, but if the ads do not infiltrate the material, this is not a reason to rule them out. For example, every television and print news source has a Web site, and some of these are perfectly fine to use as source material. However, because many news sources are also involved in entertainment, the material should still be validated.

A Word to the Wise

In general, you should always use your common sense when considering the information on any Web site as a source for your research. Just because something is on the Internet doesn't mean that it is reliable or even factual. It is absolutely essential that you thoroughly authenticate each Web site and the information on it before you use the information and cite the site and writer as a source.

WHAT ABOUT WIKIPEDIA?

If you've ever surfed the Web, it's likely you have encountered the Web site Wikipedia (www.wikipedia.org). According to the Web site itself, Wikipedia is "a free, Web-based, collaborative, multilingual encyclopedia project supported by the nonprofit Wikimedia Foundation." Basically, Wikipedia is an online encyclopedia with articles on millions of topics in a variety of languages. All you need to do is type in a word in Wikipedia's search box and you're likely to find an article about it.

However, unlike traditional encyclopedias that are written and edited by experts, the articles on Wikipedia can be written and edited by anyone who visits the Web site. Not surprisingly, this means that information on Wikipedia is incomplete, incorrect, biased, or has no or few sources to support it.

Because of its open-editing policy, many instructors and professors ban the use of Wikipedia as a source for research papers. It would definitely be a mistake to assume that anything found on Wikipedia is factual. However, a certain amount of the information on Wikipedia is useful.

Many students find that Wikipedia provides a good starting point for research, especially on unfamiliar topics. They look up a topic, get the basic idea, and then look for more varied, deeper sources of information. Another way to use Wikipedia is to find some information that seems factual and then try to find additional sources that back it up.

Just keep in mind that every "fact" you find on Wikipedia must be backed up with other sources. You don't necessarily need to avoid Wikipedia entirely, but you do need to use it with caution—as a first step only.

HOW TO AVOID PLAGIARISM

The definition of plagiarism includes the term common knowledge. To help you figure out what information you need to cite in your research papers, you first need to become familiar with what common knowledge is. This is information that everyone generally knows or that can be found easily in a variety of sources. For example, the fact that Madrid is the capital of Spain is considered common knowledge. Generally, if something can be verified by more than three sources, it is considered common knowledge. However, if you have any doubt about whether something is common knowledge, you should cite your source.

Paraphrasing and Summarizing

As a general rule, you should use quotations sparingly in your writing. Use quotations, for example, to illustrate a point or to provide evidence to support a point. A paper full of quotes often looks cumbersome and doesn't tell the reader very much about your own analysis.

Paraphrasing is one way to avoid the overuse of quotations. Putting information in your own words also helps you learn the information. To paraphrase, you need to understand what you are reading.

Paraphrasing doesn't mean changing one or two words and keeping the rest of the material the same. That counts as plagiarism. To paraphrase, first read the information to understand the main point and supporting details and then write what you learned from memory. Next, reread your version against the original material to make sure you have not copied anything directly or misstated the author's point or evidence.

Another option is to summarize, which involves choosing only the most important details from a work and writing them in your own words. However, even when you paraphrase or summarize, you still need to cite the source.

Keeping Records of Your Sources

It's important to document your sources, so be sure to keep a record of all the reference materials you use. You should copy or print out every original source—whether print or online—even if you're not sure you'll use it in your paper. Make sure that in your notes you differentiate between common knowledge, opinions, quotations, paraphrases, and summaries. This way you will avoid leaving out the appropriate quotation marks or citation.

Make sure to proofread your paper carefully. You can read it over once for clarity and a second time for proper citations. Remember that if you fail to cite your sources properly, you could be considered guilty of plagiarism.

NOTE: If you are stating your own opinion in a paper, you don't need to cite yourself as the source. However, you should always back up your opinion with information from sources—which you cite.

HOW TO CITE REFERENCES CORRECTLY

You have your references and you're ready to write. So how should you cite your sources? There is no easy answer to that question because there are several formats.

Parenthetical Citations

In the body of a paper, writers can use parenthetical citations or footnotes and endnotes. With parenthetical citations, the information about the source is located in parentheses at the end of a sentence, for example,

> "Yet at this time, the notion of cities began to change throughout the industrialized world." (Watanabe, 2003).

This shows the reader who the author is and the year the source was written. There are some variations on the parenthetical citation shown in the next section.

Citing sources this way is helpful to readers because they know immediately where the information came from. If readers want to know more about the source, they can refer to the bibliography at the end of your paper. This is a complete list of every source used in your paper. The list of sources includes more specific information about the authors, titles, and publications. This list is arranged alphabetically by the author's surname or by the title of the work if no author is listed.

Footnotes and Endnotes

Two other formats for citing sources are endnotes and footnotes. Instead of putting your citation information in parentheses after the sentence, you add a superscript number each time you quote, paraphrase, or summarize information. The number corresponds to a citation at the bottom of the page (for footnotes) or at the end of your paper (for endnotes):

"Yet at this time, the notion of cities began to change throughout the industrialized world."[1]

[1]Peter Watanabe, *Today and Tomorrow*, (Hatfield: Hatfield Press, 2003), 209

When using footnotes or endnotes, you still need to include a bibliography at the end of your paper.

Citation Styles

There are a few different citation styles commonly used in academia. Your instructor will likely tell you which citation style you are expected to use for your class assignments.

Here are the three main citation styles and how they differ:

American Psychological Association (APA) Style

APA is one of the most common styles used in academic writing and is generally found in works in the social sciences such as psychology and economics. In APA style, citations are placed within sentences and paragraphs. The last name of the author, the year of publication, and the page number are included.

throughout the industrialized world (Watanabe, 2003, p. 254).

If the name of the author appears as part of the text, you would only need to cite the date in parentheses:

Watanabe (2003) argues that . . .

Modern Language Association (MLA) Style

The MLA style is another very commonly used style in academia, generally in the humanities such as history and literature. Like

APA style, MLA style uses in-text <u>citations</u>. MLA requires only the author's last name and page number within the text.

throughout the industrialized world (Watanabe 254).

Chicago Manual of Style

The Chicago style is less popular then MLA and APA styles in academia, thought it is used at many universities across the country and in textbooks. There are a few different types of Chicago style for <u>citations</u>, but here is the most common Chicago author–date <u>citation</u>:

throughout the industrialized world (Watanabe 2003).

Bibliographical Citations

Each style also has its own way to cite sources in a <u>bibliography</u> at the end of your research paper. Your instructors will likely tell you which style they prefer you use and will direct you to the proper handbooks or Web sites to guide you through the process.

A Final Word to the Wise

To reiterate: Keep track of your sources by making copies of them if they are print materials or by printing them out if they are online. It is usually too hard after your paper has been written to go back and find the sources you have used. If you keep a record of the sources you consult from the beginning, you'll be more able to cite the correct sources and to cite them correctly.

CITING ONLINE REFERENCES

Not surprisingly, you'll need to cite your online references in your papers and your bibliographies. Like citing a print source, you need to include the author, title, and date, but there are a few differences, including inclusion of the URL where you found the information and the date when you accessed it. Each style (APA, MLA, and Chicago) has its own way to cite different online references, such as journal articles, magazine articles, and Web sites in general. Your instructor should provide you with detailed instructions, but here are examples of how to cite a magazine article in each style:

APA
Kirejczyk, C. (November 17, 2006). The Future of Online Learning. *The Trylon*. Retrieved from http://www.Web site. title.

MLA
Kirejczyk, Christopher. "The Future of Online Learning." *The Trylon*. November 17, 2006. March 14, 2010 .

Chicago
Kirejczyk, Christopher. "The Future of Online Learning." *The Trylon*, November 17, 2006, http://www.Web site.title (accessed March 14, 2010).

▶ IS THIS ONLINE SOURCE RELIABLE? CHECKLIST

When conducting research on the Internet, you are confronted with a vast amount of material. Some sources are completely credible, whereas others are completely unreliable. If you have any doubts about the validity of your online source, ask yourself the following questions:

☐ Am I able to tell what organization is responsible for the information on the site?

☐ What do I know about this organization (or can find out)?

☐ Is there a link to a page that clearly defines what the organization does (i.e., an "About Us" or "Mission" page)?

☐ Is there valid contact information on the organization's Web site?

☐ Can I easily figure out who authored the information?

☐ What do I know about this person (or can find out)?

☐ Is there a date on the articles on the Web site indicating when they were written?

☐ Does the Web site include cited sources, linked if possible?

☐ Is the Web site free of grammatical and spelling errors?

☐ Does the writing on the Web site seem balanced and unbiased?

☐ If there are advertisements on the Web site, are they separate from the content?

If you answered "no" to any of these questions, you may want to rethink using this source.

▶Part IV

APPENDIX

Search

Appendix `Go`

Some Online Learning Terms You Should Know

A

accredited: certified as meeting certain standards by a regional or professional association

adware: program that is secretly installed on computers to open pop-up ads and redirect Internet searches to advertising sites

ANGEL: a type of management system used to deliver online courses

antispyware software: software designed to eliminate spyware on a computer system

antivirus software: software used to prevent, detect, and remove computer viruses

asynchronous: not occurring or existing at the same time; type of online course

audio chat: an application that enables two or more users to carry on an oral exchange over the Internet

B

baud rate: a measure of signal changes per second; used to rate the speed of a modem

bibliography: a list of source materials that appears at the end of a paper, article, chapter, or book in which the materials were cited

Blackboard: a type of management system used by online schools to deliver courses

blended learning: a type of learning that combines the online delivery of materials with traditional teaching methods such as in-person lectures or discussions

C

chat room: a site on the Internet where a number of users can communicate in real time

citation: short documentation of the source of the information used in a report, presentation, speech

closed-captioning: a technology that adds text captions to a video; used to assist the hearing-impaired

common knowledge: something which is generally known by a large number of people and accepted as fact

correspondence course: a course in which materials are delivered back and forth through postal mail; early form of distance learning

D

diploma mill: a fraudulent business that awards academic degrees and diplomas in exchange for money; students do no work for the degrees

discussion board: an online "bulletin board" where users leave messages and read and reply to messages left by others

dissertation: a publication of original research that is required for a doctoral degree

distance learning: learning where the instructor and the students are in physically separate locations

DSL: digital subscriber line; DSL provides data transmission over the wires of a local telephone network

E

e-book: electronic book; a book that has been digitized and is available online

external disk drive: drive attached manually outside the hard drive to play or record on CDs or DVDs

F

FAFSA (Free Application for Federal Student Aid): form required for federal, state, and school-sponsored financial aid programs

financial aid: funding intended to help students pay expenses for education at a college or university

G

grant: an award of financial assistance that does not have to be repaid

H

<u>hybrid learning</u>: see blended learning

I

<u>instant messaging, IM</u>: a type of real-time communication in which users type text to one another online

<u>Internet Service Provider, ISP</u>: a company that offers its customers access to the Internet

L

<u>live chat</u>: any kind of real-time communication over the Internet, though usually referring to text-based chat

<u>loan forgiveness</u>: a program in which the federal government will cancel or "forgive" all or part of an educational loan in exchange for volunteer work, military service, or other criteria

M

<u>media player</u>: a software program that allows you to play audio and video files

<u>memory stick</u>: external device used to save files and programs residing on the hard drive

<u>message board</u>: an online discussion site on which messages are posted and users can reply to posted messages

Moodle: a type of management system used to deliver online courses

multimedia presentation: a presentation that can involve a combination of any of the following: text, audio, still images, or video

O

online learning: distance learning in which most of the instruction is delivered via the Internet

P

paraphrase: to restate the ideas of another person in your own words

PDF reader: a program used to open PDF (portable document format) files. PDF is a file format that captures all the elements of a printed document as an electronic image

Pell Grant: awarded by the federal government, based on financial need; maximum amount of grants determined by federal law; both undergraduate and graduate students may be eligible

plagiarism, plagiarize: to use the words and thoughts of another author, but represent them as your own original work

podcast: an audio broadcast that has been converted to an audio file format for playback

pop-up ad: type of ad found on the Internet that opens automatically on-screen; can be unknowingly downloaded to a computer while browsing the Internet

pop-up blocker: blocks certain pop-up ads from opening

S

scholarship: financial aid provided to a student on the basis of academic merit; no repayment is required

screen reader: a software program that reads the contents of the screen aloud to a user; for users with impaired vision

self-study class: an online learning class in which students download materials and work at their own pace without guidance from an instructor

Stafford Loan: fixed-interest-rate loan for undergraduate and graduate students; may be need-based or not

syllabus: an outline or summary of topics that will be covered during an academic course

synchronous: occurring or existing at the same time; form of online course

system unit: core of a computer consisting of the processor and memory

T

teleconference: two-way electronic communication between two or more groups in separate locations via audio and/or video software

text chat: a conversation through text messages, either through text messaging systems on the Internet or by mobile phone

threaded discussion: a form of asynchronous discussion on the Internet; one user posts a message or a document and other users respond to it in their own time

transcript(s): a list of the courses a student has taken and the grades that he or she earned

tutorial: step-by-step instructions presented through Web-based technology; designed to teach a user how to perform a particular action

V

video chat: participation in a Webcam-based discussion between two or more people

video lecture: a lecture presented by an instructor viewed online via a media player

virtual classroom: a learning environment in which instructors and students are separated by time, space, or both, and the instructor provides course content via the Internet

voice chat: see audio chat

W

Web camera or Web cam: video-capture device connected to a computer, permitting the computer to act as a videophone

Webcast: a video and/or audio broadcast transmitted via the Internet

Webinar: a Web seminar, used to conduct live meetings or presentations over the Internet

NOTES

NOTES

NOTES

NOTES

NOTES

NOTES